Better Homes and Gardens.

CELEBRATE THE RED, WHITE & BLUE

✳

101 PATRIOTIC CRAFTS, FOOD & DECORATING IDEAS

Better Homes and Gardens® Books
Des Moines, Iowa

★

Better Homes and Gardens® Books
An imprint of Meredith® Books

CELEBRATE THE RED, WHITE & BLUE

Editor: Carol Field Dahlstrom
Contributing Editor: Susan M. Banker
Graphic Designer: Angela Haupert Hoogensen
Contributing Researcher: Judy Bailey
Copy Chief: Terri Fredrickson
Editorial Operations Manager: Karen Schirm
Managers, Book Production: Pam Kvitne, Marjorie J. Schenkelberg
Contributing Proofreaders: Maria Duryée, Gretchen Kauffman, M. Peg Smith
Technical Illustrator: Chris Neubauer Graphics, Inc.
Electronic Production Coordinator: Paula Forest
Editorial and Design Assistants: Kaye Chabot, Mary Lee Gavin
Contributing Designers: Susan M. Banker, Donna and Gaylen Chesnut,
Phyllis Dunstan, Pam Kvitne, Barbara Sestok, Margaret Sindelar, Alice Wetzel
Photography: Andy Lyons Cameraworks, Scott Little
Stock Photography: Comstock Inc.

Meredith® Books
Editor in Chief: James D. Blume
Design Director: Matt Strelecki
Managing Editor: Gregory H. Kayko

Director, Sales, Special Markets: Rita McMullen
Director, Sales, Premiums: Michael A. Peterson
Director, Sales, Retail: Tom Wierzbicki
Director, Book Marketing: Brad Elmitt
Director, Operations: George A. Susral
Director, Production: Douglas M. Johnston

Vice President and General Manager: Douglas J. Guendel

Better Homes and Gardens® Magazine
Editor in Chief: Karol DeWulf Nickell

Meredith Publishing Group
President, Publishing Group: Stephen M. Lacy
Vice President-Publishing Director: Bob Mate

Meredith Corporation
Chairman and Chief Executive Officer: William T. Kerr

Chairman of the Executive Committee: E. T. Meredith III

Copyright © 2002 by Meredith Corporation, Des Moines, Iowa. First Edition.
All rights reserved. Printed in the United States of America.
Library of Congress Control Number: 2001134082
(Hardcover) ISBN: 0-696-21571-3 (Softcover) ISBN: 0-696-21538-1

All of us at Better Homes and Gardens® Books are dedicated to providing you with information and ideas to create beautiful and useful projects. We welcome your comments and suggestions. Write to us at: Better Homes and Gardens Books, Crafts Editorial Department, 1716 Locust Street—LN112, Des Moines, IA 50309-3023.

If you would like to purchase any of our crafts, cooking, gardening, home improvement, or home decorating and design books, check wherever quality books are sold. Or visit us at bhgbooks.com

★

CONTENTS

FROM THE EDITOR

We stand and put our hands on our hearts as it is carried by men and women in uniform at parades. We salute and sing as it is raised at sporting events and other gatherings. We catch a glimpse of it as it hangs quietly on front porches and on tall rural poles as we go about our daily work. Our flag is a symbol of everything we cherish in the United States of America. As we salute its broad stripes and bright stars, it is there to remind us of our freedom and the struggles we have endured. Many of us remember with great emotion the image of a little boy waving the flag at his father's funeral in 1963. We also have a clear memory of an American astronaut proudly placing our flag on the moon, taking a giant step for mankind. And many of us have sadly experienced being handed the American flag, folded so neatly into a triangle, as "Taps" is played and guns fire in the distance.

Whether present at a time of ceremony, celebration, or grieving, the flag serves as a symbol of strength, reminding us to hold fast to the patriotic dreams of our forefathers and to remember those who died in the name of freedom. It makes us proud to touch, display, and wear the colors so dear to us. By sharing this national spirit our patriotism grows stronger and our nation becomes more united.

Our flag, and what it stands for, can be celebrated in so many ways. Whether we wear our colors to show pride, display red, white, and blue throughout our homes, make a gift to celebrate an all-American occasion, or think about our country's flag as we prepare meals for our families and friends, we show national spirit and love of freedom to those around us.

Within this book, we hope you'll find ideas to show your love for the great American flag, and that your patriotism grows every day as you celebrate the Red, White, and Blue.

Carol Field Dahlstrom

CELEBRATING OLD GLORY

Did you know that our flag was once called Old Glory? After the signing of the Declaration of Independence on July 4, 1776, Americans wanted a national flag to replace the many individual banners associated with various regiments. To symbolize the union of the states, the Continental Congress adopted the following resolution on June 14, 1777:

"Resolved: that the flag of the United States be thirteen stripes, alternate red and white; that the union be thirteen stars, white in a blue field, representing a new constellation."

Because the resolution was vague, the flags that followed were varied by each flagmaker. For the next 135 years, the United States flag officially changed 24 times. The 50th star on today's flag was added on July 4, 1960. All United States flags, whatever the

design, are valid and may be flown. These historic flags deserve the same honor and respect given today's flag.

The term "Old Glory" was coined by Captain Stephen Driver, a shipmaster of Salem, Massachusetts. As he was leaving on one of his many voyages in 1831, friends presented him with a 24-star flag. As the flag opened to the ocean breeze, he exclaimed "Old Glory!"

In 1837 the captain retired to Nashville, taking his treasured flag with him. By the time the Civil War erupted, most everyone in and around Nashville recognized Captain Driver's "Old Glory." When Tennessee seceded from the Union, rebels were determined to destroy his flag; however, repeated searches revealed no trace of it.

On February 25, 1862, Union forces captured Nashville and raised the American flag over the capitol. It was a small flag, and immediately people began asking Captain Driver whether Old Glory still existed. Happy to have soldiers with him this time, Driver went home and ripped at the seams of his bedcover to reveal his original Old Glory.

Captain Driver gently gathered up the flag and returned with the soldiers to the capitol. Although he was 60 years old, the captain climbed up to the tower to replace the smaller banner with his beloved flag. The Sixth Ohio Regiment cheered and saluted, and later adopted the nickname Old Glory as their own, telling and retelling the story of Driver's devotion to the flag we continue to honor.

Captain Driver's grave in the old Nashville City Cemetery is one of three places authorized by an act of Congress where the United States flag may be flown 24 hours a day.

PATRIOTIC
ACCENTS

✶

ALL THROUGH
THE HOUSE

MEMORY ALBUM

LAYERED PAPERS, ANTIQUING GEL, AND A TREASURED PHOTOGRAPH
PROVIDE A VINTAGE APPEARANCE TO THIS ALBUM COVER. THIS IS THE
PERFECT PROJECT TO SHOW OFF PATRIOTIC PHOTOGRAPHS, POSTCARDS,
STAMPS, LETTERS, AND OTHER HEARTWARMING MEMORABILIA.

WHAT YOU'LL NEED

★ *Photo album or scrapbook*
★ *Newspapers*
★ *White spray primer*
★ *Textured lightweight papers,
such as tissue paper, in white,
red, and blue*
★ *Paintbrush*
★ *Glossy decoupage medium*
★ *Tracing paper*
★ *Pencil*
★ *Scissors*
★ *Heavy textured ivory or
white paper*
★ *Photograph*
★ *Cardboard*
★ *Photo spray adhesive*
★ *Brown antiquing gel*
★ *Soft cloth*

HERE'S HOW

1 Remove the pages from the album. In a well-ventilated work area, lay the book flat, cover side up, on a newspaper-covered work surface. Spray the book with white primer. Let the paint dry.

2 Tear strips of red and blue paper into shapes.

3 Using a paintbrush, spread a generous amount of decoupage medium onto the book cover. Cover the book cover with white paper first. Paint decoupage medium over the white paper. Layer blue paper strips in the upper left corner. Using the photograph, *opposite*, as a guide, layer the red paper on the book, and paint decoupage medium over it. The papers should extend beyond the edges at least ½ inch. Let the decoupage medium dry.

4 Trace the stars onto tracing paper and cut them out. Trace around the large star once and the small star twice onto heavy textured paper. Cut out stars. Decoupage the stars on the cover.

5 For the cover photograph, use an original, photocopy, or computer-print of a photo. Trim the photo to the desired size. Spray the back of the photo with photo adhesive. Affix it to colored cardboard or heavy cardstock. Spray adhesive on the back to affix it to the album cover. Coat the surface of the photo album, including the photo, with decoupage medium.

6 Trim the paper around the edge of the book, allowing approximately ⅜ inch to extend beyond the edges. Fold the paper over the edge and decoupage it in place. Let the medium dry.

7 Paint a thin coat of antiquing gel over the surface of the album cover. Wipe gently with a damp cloth. Let the antiquing dry.

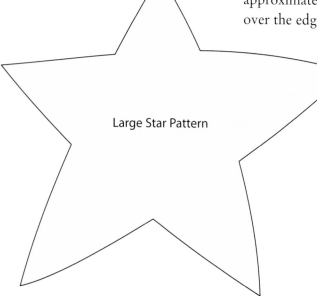

Large Star Pattern

Small Star Pattern

PLAYFULLY PATRIOTIC

★

SHOW YOUR PRIDE FOR AMERICA WITH THIS COLORFUL FRONT DOOR DECORATION. PAINTED EARS OF CORN ARE AN UNEXPECTED TWIST TO THE SYMBOLIC RED, WHITE, AND BLUE.

WHAT YOU'LL NEED

- ★ 5 ears of corn
- ★ Bleach and water
- ★ Cloth
- ★ Tape
- ★ White spray primer
- ★ Acrylic paints in red, white, and blue
- ★ Paintbrushes
- ★ Gold spray paint
- ★ Red cord

HERE'S HOW

1. Soften, clean, and shape the ears of corn by soaking them in ¼ cup bleach and 1 gallon of water. Carefully pull back the husks and shape into an arrangement. Wipe off the ears of corn and set them aside until husks dry.

2. Wrap cloth around the husks and secure it with tape. In a well-ventilated work area, spray ears of corn with white spray primer. Let the primer dry.

3. Using the photograph, *opposite,* for ideas, paint the ears or corn as desired. Let the paint dry.

4. Cover the painted corn with cloth and secure it with tape next to husks. Spray the husks gold. Let the paint dry.

5. Arrange the corn and tie a red cord around the bundle.

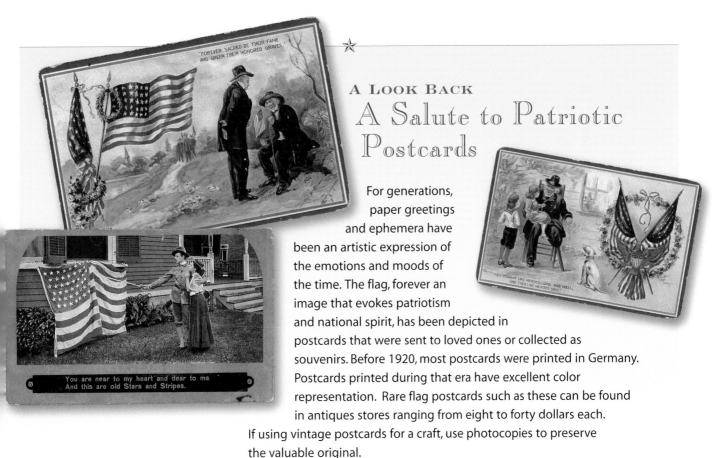

A LOOK BACK
A Salute to Patriotic Postcards

For generations, paper greetings and ephemera have been an artistic expression of the emotions and moods of the time. The flag, forever an image that evokes patriotism and national spirit, has been depicted in postcards that were sent to loved ones or collected as souvenirs. Before 1920, most postcards were printed in Germany. Postcards printed during that era have excellent color representation. Rare flag postcards such as these can be found in antiques stores ranging from eight to forty dollars each. If using vintage postcards for a craft, use photocopies to preserve the valuable original.

MUSICAL TRIBUTE WREATH

THE GRAND OL' FLAG PROUDLY FLIES IN THIS MUSIC-THEME WREATH, WHILE MUSIC NOTE TRIMS DANCE AROUND PATRIOTIC SONG SHEETS.

WHAT YOU'LL NEED

★ *5 copies of antique patriotic music, photocopied on parchment paper*
★ *Hot-glue gun; hotmelt adhesive*
★ *13 each small ball ornaments in red, silver, and blue*
★ *Black pipe cleaners; scissors*
★ *32-inch grapevine wreath*
★ *12×17-inch United States flag on wood stick*
★ *Two 6-inch musical note ornaments*
★ *One 6-inch G clef ornament*
★ *4 yards each of 1½-inch-wide sheer ribbon in red, white, and blue*
★ *Two 5-inch glittered stars each in red, white, and blue*

HERE'S HOW

1 Roll four of the music sheets so the titles are visible. Glue to secure. Curl the upper left corner of the remaining sheet. Set aside.

2 Cut the string hangers from the ball ornaments. Make 13 groups of one red, one white, and one blue ornaments. Slide a pipe cleaner through the wire hangers and twist to secure. Set aside.

3 Align the ribbon ends. Tie a large bow in the center. Hot-glue the bow to the upper left of the wreath.

4 Cut the hangers from the musical note ornaments. Arrange embellishments on the wreath, using the photograph, *opposite*, as a guide. To secure the ball ornament bundles, poke the pipe cleaners through the wreath to the back, and twist them around the wreath. Trim the pipe cleaner ends. Hot-glue the remaining pieces on the wreath.

A LOOK BACK

A Salute to Our National Anthem

Francis Scott Key, a respected lawyer, lived in Georgetown from about 1804 to 1833. During the war of 1812, Key learned that his friend, Dr. William Beanes, was held prisoner on a British warship. Key and another friend boarded the ship, armed with letters of praise written by British patients under Beanes' care. Although the British agreed to release the doctor, they held all three captive until after the battle ended to prevent the Americans from revealing plans of attack to the patriots on shore. At Fort McHenry, the commander asked for a flag so big that "the British would have no trouble seeing it from a distance." On September 13, 1814, the British began bombarding Baltimore. The Americans watched the battle and waited for the sign that would end their anxiety. When daylight came, the flag was still there! An amateur poet, Key was inspired to write "The Star Spangled Banner." On March 3, 1931, it was adopted as our national anthem.

STAR-SPANGLED BOX

EMBELLISH A STAR-SHAPE BOX WITH THE WORDS FROM THE NATIONAL ANTHEM. WRITTEN INTO TEXTURED GEL, THE WORDS OF FRANCIS SCOTT KEY WILL BE CHERISHED FOR GENERATIONS.

WHAT YOU'LL NEED

- ★ *Pencil*
- ★ *Ruled notebook paper*
- ★ *Scissors*
- ★ *Star-shape box*
- ★ *Texturizing gel (found in acrylic paint section of art stores)*
- ★ *Palette knife*
- ★ *Acrylic paints in cream, blue, and red*
- ★ *Paintbrush*
- ★ *Glossy decoupage medium*
- ★ *Brown antiquing gel*
- ★ *Rag*

HERE'S HOW

1 Write out the first verse of "The Star-Spangled Banner" (see one version, *below*) on a piece of lined notebook paper. Cut out each line and arrange onto the box lid to fit. Keeping in order, set aside the words for reference later. Use a ruler to draw pencil lines on box lid to use as a guide for each line of words.

2 Use a palette knife to spread texturizing gel onto the lid surface one line at a time, spreading evenly to the pencil drawn baseline. The gel is usually white and dries transparent. Write the words into the gel with a sharp pencil or other instrument until all lines are completed.

3 Spread gel on lid sides. Let the gel dry.

4 Place the lid on the box. Draw a line around the box along the edge of the lid. Remove the lid. Spread gel onto box sides below the pencil line. Draw lines to divide stripes. Let the gel dry.

5 Paint the lid top and the sides of the box cream. Paint the lid sides blue. Paint alternating red stripes on the box sides. Let the paint dry.

6 Paint a coat of decoupage medium onto the entire surface. Let it dry.

7 Paint brown antiquing gel onto painted surfaces. When it begins to dry, wipe it with a slightly dampened soft cloth, removing some of the gel and leaving brown in the crevices. Let the gel dry.

O, say can you see
By the dawn's early light,
What so proudly we hailed at the twilight's last gleaming?
Whose broad stripes and bright stars, thro' the perilous fight
O'er the ramparts we watched, were so gallantly streaming.
And the rockets' red glare, the bombs bursting in air,
Gave proof thro' the night that our flag was still there.
O say, does that star-spangled banner yet wave
O'er the land of the free and the home of the brave?

O say,
can you see
by the dawn's
early light what so proudly we
hailed at the twilight's last gleaming? Whose broad
stripes and bright stars, thro' the perilous fight
o'er the ramparts we watched, were so
gallantly streaming? And the rockets' red
glare, the bombs bursting in air,
gave proof thro' the night that
our flag was still there.
O say does that Star-Spangled
Banner yet wave o'er the land
of the free and the home of the brave?

FREEDOM FRAMES

★

PATRIOTIC POSTAGE STAMPS ADD PERSONALITY AND HISTORY
TO PURCHASED MATS AND FRAMES. USE THIS EASY DECOUPAGE
TECHNIQUE TO SHOWCASE FAMILY MILITARY PHOTOGRAPHS,
LETTERS, AND HONORS.

WHAT YOU'LL NEED

★ *New or cancelled postage
stamps (not self-stick, available
in crafts stores and hobby shops)*
★ *Frame or picture mat*
★ *Decoupage medium*
★ *Paintbrush*

HERE'S HOW

1 If necessary, remove paper backing from the stamps (see *below*).
2 Arrange the stamps on a picture frame or mat. Using a paintbrush,
  apply decoupage medium to the back of each stamp. Glue the
  stamps on the mat or picture frame until a desired look is achieved.
  Let the glue dry.

★

A LOOK BACK
Patriotic Stamps

Collections of U.S. postage stamps reveal much about
our country's history. From the first official U.S.
government postage stamp of 1847 to those
purchased and used today, stamps reflect the
heritage, leaders, triumphs, passions, and
philosophies of the country.

When using vintage stamps for crafts and
decorating, check the value of the stamp before using.
Set aside rare, valuable stamps.

Post offices and some crafts supply stores sell a variety of stamps.
Or, collect used stamps by removing them from envelopes. To remove
stamps, tear or cut off the upper right-hand corner of the envelope. Soak
it, stamp side down, in warm water. Once the stamp falls away from the
paper, let it soak for a few minutes more to remove any remaining glue
on the stamp. Pick up the stamp with tongs and dry it between paper
towels. Place it under a heavy book for several hours. If the stamp will not
peel away from the paper backing, trim around the stamp using
decorative-edge scissors.

STAND-UP STARS

STARS, WITH THEIR JUTTING POINTS, ARE EYE-CATCHING SHAPES.
THIS COLLECTION OF WOOD STARS IS NO EXCEPTION.
PAINTED IN ANTIQUE TOY COLORS, SOME OF THE STARS ARE
TRIMMED WITH VINTAGE BUTTONS, TORN-FABRIC BOWS,
AND TWISTED WIRE. TURN THE PAGE FOR THE PATTERNS
AND INSTRUCTIONS.

WHAT YOU'LL NEED

- ★ *Tracing paper*
- ★ *Pencil*
- ★ *Scissors*
- ★ *½- to 1-inch-thick pine*
- ★ *Band saw*
- ★ *Sandpaper*
- ★ *Tack cloth*
- ★ *Newspapers*
- ★ *Acrylic paints in red, off-white, and blue*
- ★ *Paintbrush*
- ★ *Wood glue*
- ★ *Thick white crafts glue*
- ★ *Buttons*
- ★ *Fabric Scraps*
- ★ *Wire and wire cutters*
- ★ *Round pencil, small dowel, or wood skewer*

HERE'S HOW

1 Trace a pattern, *opposite,* onto tracing paper. To trace the half-star pattern, fold tracing paper in half. Align the paper and pattern folds and trace the star. Cut out the star and unfold the tracing paper. Transfer the pattern to the wood.

2 Using a band saw, carefully cut on the pattern lines. Sand the edges smooth. Wipe away dust with a tack cloth.

3 Cover the work area with newspapers. Paint one side and the edges of the star. Let the paint dry. Turn the star over and paint the other side. Let it dry. Apply a second coat if needed. Let the paint dry.

4 Sand the edges of the star again to provide a weathered look. Remove dust from sanding with a tack cloth.

5 If desired, layer a small star on a larger star, referring to the photograph on *pages 18–19* as a guide. Glue the stars together with wood glue. Let the glue dry.

6 For the button stars, use thick white crafts glue to glue a button to the center of the star. Let the glue dry. Layer and glue two or three buttons or glue several small buttons on the star.

7 For the bow star, tear a strip from fabric, approximately 1×12 inches. Place the fabric strip across the back of the star. Tie the fabric strip into a bow on the front of the star. Glue the bow in place, if desired, and trim the ends.

8 For the wire-wrapped star, wrap a long length of wire around the center of the star. Twist the wire ends together to secure. Trim the ends of the wire, leaving about 3 inches on each end. To coil the ends, wrap the wire ends around a pencil, small dowel, or wood skewer.

"The future belongs to those who believe in the beauty of their dreams."

— FIRST LADY ELEANOR ROOSEVELT

Star Patterns

CROCHETED STARS

THESE QUICKLY CROCHETED STARS ARE JUST THE RIGHT SIZE
TO ADORN CHRISTMAS TREE BRANCHES OR TO TIE ATOP FESTIVELY
WRAPPED GIFT PACKAGES.

WHAT YOU'LL NEED

★ *DMC pearl cotton thread,*
size 5, in assorted colors
★ *Size 4 steel crochet hook*

ABBREVIATIONS

beg = beginning
ch = chain
dc = double crochet
rep = repeat
rnd = round
sc = single crochet
sk = skip
sl st = slip stitch
sp = space
st = stitch
* = repeat whatever follows
the * as indicated
( ) = work directions in
parentheses the number of
times specified

Finished stars measure
4¹/₂ inches wide.

HERE'S HOW

1 **CENTER:** Using a double strand of thread throughout, ch 5, join with sl st to form ring. **Rnd 1:** Ch 3, dc in ring, (ch 2, 2 dc in ring) 4 times; ch 2, join with sl st to top of beg ch-3. **Rnd 2:** Sl st in next dc and ch-2 sp; ch 3, dc in same sp, ch 2, 2 dc in same sp = first corner shell made; (ch 1, in next ch-2 sp make shell of 2 dc, ch 2, 2 dc) 4 times; ch 1, join with sl st to top of beg ch-3. **Rnd 3:** Sl st in next dc and ch-2 sp; ch 3 and make a first corner shell; ch 1, 2 dc in next ch-1 sp, ch 1, (shell in next ch-2 sp, ch 1, 2 dc in next ch-1 sp, ch 1) 4 times. Join with sl st to top of beg ch-3. Fasten off.

2 **POINT: Row 1:** Attach thread in any ch-2 corner sp, ch 1, sc in same sp, (sc in next 2 dc and ch-sp) 3 times, ch 3, sl st in third ch from hook = point made; turn. **Rows 2-8:** Sk first sc, sc across; ch 3, sl st in third ch from hook; turn. **Row 9:** Sk first sc, sl st in next sc. Fasten off. Rep rows 1-9 four times around. Weave in all ends.

OLD GLORY EVERGREEN

ORNAMENTS IN THE COLORS OF OLD GLORY CLEVERLY COVER THE
BRANCHES OF THIS CHRISTMAS TREE.

WHAT YOU'LL NEED FOR THE CROCHETED CANDY CANES

★ *J&P Coats Speed-Cro-Sheen (100 yard ball): one ball each of white (1) and Spanish red (126)*
★ *Size D crochet hook*
★ *One 6-inch length of gold cord*
★ *One 12-inch chenille stem*
★ *Yarn needle*

WHAT YOU'LL NEED FOR THE SCULPTED STARS

★ *Package of white modeling compound , such as Sculpey (makes three ornaments)*
★ *Waxed paper; rolling pin*
★ *Star cookie cutter*
★ *Miniature cookie cutters*
★ *Assorted diameter straws*
★ *Sharp knife (optional)*
★ *Clear acrylic spray; monofilament*

HERE'S HOW TO MAKE THE CROCHETED CANDY CANES

1 **Red Coil:** Ch 63. Work 3 sc in fourth ch from hook and in each ch across. Fasten off.
2 **White Coil:** Work as for Red Coil. Fasten off, leaving an 8-inch strand.
3 Weave in loose ends except for the strand. Trim chenille stem to 8½ inches, then fold up ¼ inch at each end. Twist the two coils around each other and the chenille stem. Bend into a cane shape. Thread strand into yarn needle and run through inside of coils; take several backstitches to secure. Tie cord around top of cane and, holding ends together, tie in an overhand knot for hanger.

HERE'S HOW TO MAKE THE SCULPTED STARS

1 Knead modeling compound until pliable. Roll between two layers of waxed paper to a ³⁄₁₆-inch thickness.
2 Using a star cutter, cut out shapes. Referring to the patterns, *page 96,* cut small shapes within star using smaller cookie cutters and straws. Use a straw only once or twice, then cut off the filled section of the straw before proceeding. A sharp knife also may be used to cut additional shapes. Bake stars on a cookie sheet at 250°F for 25 to 30 minutes. Cool completely; spray with a coating of clear acrylic. Hang with monofilament.

LOVE-MY-COUNTRY LINENS

ADD EVEN MORE FLARE TO YOUR FOURTH OF JULY CELEBRATION WITH
RED, WHITE, AND BLUE PLACE MAT AND NAPKIN SETS. THIS PATRIOTIC
PAIR, USING MOSTLY WHOLE STITCHES, IS A GREAT BEGINNER PROJECT.

WHAT YOU'LL NEED
FOR ONE PLACE SETTING

★ *12×18½-inch piece of
14-count Aida*
★ *15×15-inch piece of
14-count Aida*
★ *Cotton embroidery floss in
colors listed in key, below*
★ *Needle; embroidery hoop*
★ *Sewing thread to match Aida cloth*

HERE'S HOW

1 Topstitch around napkin or place mat ½ inch from the raw edges.
Measure 1½ inches from topstitching at lower left corner of napkin
or upper left corner of place mat; begin stitching center of design
there.

2 Use two plies of embroidery floss to work cross-stitches. Work
backstitches using one ply of floss.

3 To fringe, remove the threads between topstitching and cut edges.
Press finished piece from the back.

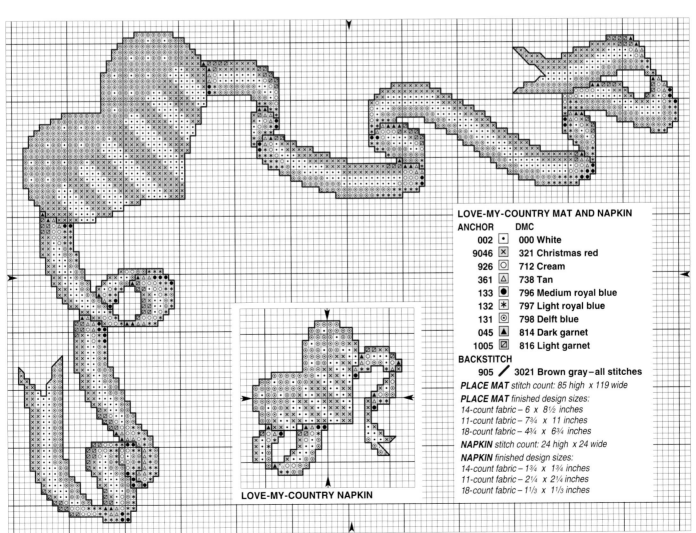

LOVE-MY-COUNTRY MAT AND NAPKIN

ANCHOR		DMC
002	•	000 White
9046	✕	321 Christmas red
926	○	712 Cream
361	△	738 Tan
133	●	796 Medium royal blue
132	✳	797 Light royal blue
131	⊙	798 Delft blue
045	▲	814 Dark garnet
1005	◪	816 Light garnet

BACKSTITCH

905	╱	3021 Brown gray – all stitches

PLACE MAT stitch count: 85 high x 119 wide
PLACE MAT finished design sizes:
14-count fabric – 6 x 8½ inches
11-count fabric – 7¾ x 11 inches
18-count fabric – 4¾ x 6¾ inches
NAPKIN stitch count: 24 high x 24 wide
NAPKIN finished design sizes:
14-count fabric – 1¾ x 1¾ inches
11-count fabric – 2¼ x 2¼ inches
18-count fabric – 1⅓ x 1⅓ inches

LOVE-MY-COUNTRY NAPKIN

LOVE-MY-COUNTRY PLACE MAT

RAZZLE-DAZZLE ACCENTS

SMALL WOOL SQUARES ARE FOLDED AND STITCHED TO PILLOW TICKING, CREATING THIS FLURRY OF PATRIOTIC FABRIC DESIGNS.

WHAT YOU'LL NEED FOR THE STAR RUG

* *1¼ yards of 45-inch-wide striped pillow-ticking fabric*
* *1 yard of fusible polyester fleece*
* *Graph paper*
* *Erasable fabric marker*
* *1½ yards of 56-inch-wide white wool fabric or equivalent scraps*
* *1¼ yards of 56-inch-wide red wool fabric or equivalent scraps*
* *1 yard of 56-inch-wide blue wool fabric or equivalent scraps*
* *Rotary cutter; cutting mat*
* *White sewing thread*
* *Liquid latex rug backing*

WHAT YOU'LL NEED FOR EACH STRIPED PILLOW

* *19×19-inch piece of fusible fleece*
* *19×19-inch square of striped pillow-ticking fabric; fabric marker*
* *½ yard of 56-inch-wide white wool fabric or equivalent in scraps*
* *½ yard of 56-inch-wide red wool fabric or equivalent in scraps*
* *½ yard of 56-inch-wide blue wool fabric or equivalent in scraps*
* *19×19-inch piece of red fabric*
* *Rotary cutter; cutting mat*
* *White sewing thread*
* *Polyester fiberfill*

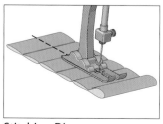

Stitching Diagram

HERE'S HOW FOR THE STAR RUG

1 Cut a 32½×43-inch rectangle from ticking and fleece. Fuse fleece to wrong side of ticking. Clean finish edges. Enlarge star pattern, *page 96*; cut out. Draw around pattern on ticking. Draw lines extending from star points to indicate blue/red color change.

2 Cut wool fabrics into 2-inch squares, using rotary cutter. Cut 752 white squares, 588 red squares, and 504 blue squares.

3 For first row, fold the two opposite edges of each of approximately 40 blue squares to center; finger-press. Pin folded squares side by side with one short edge aligned to ticking stripe 2½ inches from the edge; leave 1½ inches on each end free. Machine-stitch squares to ticking, sewing across center of each folded square. (See diagram, *below.*)

4 Finger-press stitched squares toward outer edge of rug. Fold and align a second row of blue squares with next row of ticking stripe; stitch. Last row of stitching should be 1½ inches from the edge.

5 Turn seam allowance to wrong side, mitering corners; whip-stitch in place. Paint back of rug with liquid latex rug backing.

HERE'S HOW FOR THE STRIPED PILLOWS

1 Fuse fleece to back of ticking. Use fabric marker to draw wavy or bunting stripe pattern on ticking, referring to patterns, *page 96*. Make wavy stripes about 5 inches wide. Make blue rectangle in bunting approximately 16×6 inches and red and white stripes about 2⅝ inches wide. Cut wool fabrics into 2-inch squares using a rotary cutter.

2 For first row, fold opposite edges of approximately 16 squares (all red for wavy pattern, 6 blue and 10 red for bunting) to the center and finger-press. Pin folded squares side by side with one short edge aligned to ticking stripe 2½ inches from edge; leave 1½ inches on each end free. Machine-stitch squares to ticking, sewing across center of each folded square. (See diagram, *left.*) Finger-press stitched squares toward outer edge of pillow. Fold and align a second row of squares with next row of ticking; stitch.

3 Add rows, changing colors as indicated by stripe markings. Last row of stitching should be 1½ inches from edge.

4 To assemble, sew pillow front to back, right sides facing, about ½ inch beyond last row of wool squares, leaving an opening for turning. Trim corners; turn right side out. Stuff pillows with fiberfill; slip-stitch the opening closed.

BLESS AMERICA BANNER

HANG THE WORDS OF IRVING BERLIN'S PATRIOTIC SONG FOR ALL TO ENJOY. THE SENTIMENTAL SCORE IS BOLDLY DISPLAYED ON A SUBTLE STARS-AND-STRIPES PAINTED BACKGROUND.

WHAT YOU'LL NEED

- ★ *Scissors*
- ★ *14×22-inch piece of primed canvas*
- ★ *Candle and match*
- ★ *Pencil*
- ★ *Tracing paper*
- ★ *Transfer paper*
- ★ *Medium flat brush*
- ★ *Acrylic paint in red, blue, and white*
- ★ *White transparent gel stain*
- ★ *Ruled notebook paper*
- ★ *Ruler or T-square; cloth*
- ★ *Brown antiquing gel*

God Bless America!
God bless America,
Land that I love.
Stand beside her and guide her
through the night
with a light from above.
From the mountains
to the prairies
to the oceans white with foam.
God bless America,
my home sweet home!
God bless America,
my home sweet home!

HERE'S HOW

1 Round off the corners of the canvas using scissors. Randomly cut several small notches along the edges.

2 Near a sink, use a burning candle to burn edges of canvas and create smoke marks. The canvas will burn easily.

3 Enlarge and trace the stars and stripes pattern, *below.* Transfer the pattern to the right side of the canvas.

4 To paint the solid blue and red stripes, thin the paints with equal parts of water. The colors should be transparent when painted on the canvas. Let dry. Paint white stars over blue background. Let dry.

5 Paint white gel over the banner center, fading out toward the edges, leaving the outer 2 inches unpainted. Let dry. Repeat if a lighter design is desired. Let dry.

6 Using the words, *left,* write the words to "God Bless America" on notebook paper to use as a placement guide. Tape the paper in position and make small, light pencil marks to indicate each base line. Remove the paper and draw in light pencil guidelines. Use a ruler or T-square to measure.

7 Lightly write in words with pencil, line for line. Write over them with blue paint pen. Let dry. Wipe off pencil marks with a damp cloth.

8 Paint brown antiquing gel around edges. While the gel is slightly damp, gently wipe off some gel, leaving more brown in the corners and on the edges. Let dry.

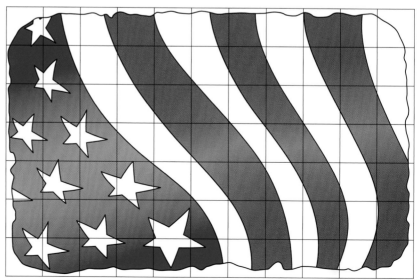

Stars and Stripes Pattern   1 Square = 1 Inch

SILVERWARE SALUTE

CELEBRATE THE RED, WHITE, AND BLUE AT A FAMILY PICNIC USING THIS PATRIOTIC FLATWARE.

WHAT YOU'LL NEED

* ★ *Purchased flatware with white plastic handles*
* ★ *¼-inch-wide masking tape*
* ★ *Binder reinforcements (available at discount and office supply stores)*
* ★ *Paint pens, such as Deco Color (available at art and crafts stores)*

HERE'S HOW

1 Wash the flatware with soap and water. Let it dry. Avoid touching the areas to be painted.

2 To make stripes on the flatware handles, wrap with pieces of masking tape. To make a solid line, burnish (rub) the edges of the masking tape. To make circles, apply binder reinforcements as desired. The covered areas will remain white after the tape or reinforcements are removed.

3 Paint the exposed areas of the flatware handles with paint pens, stroking the paint in one direction. Let the paint dry. Repeat if necessary. Remove the masking tape or reinforcements. If necessary, clean up uneven edges using the pens. Let the paint dry.

To clean painted flatware: Avoid soaking in water. Handwash the flatware and gently towel dry.

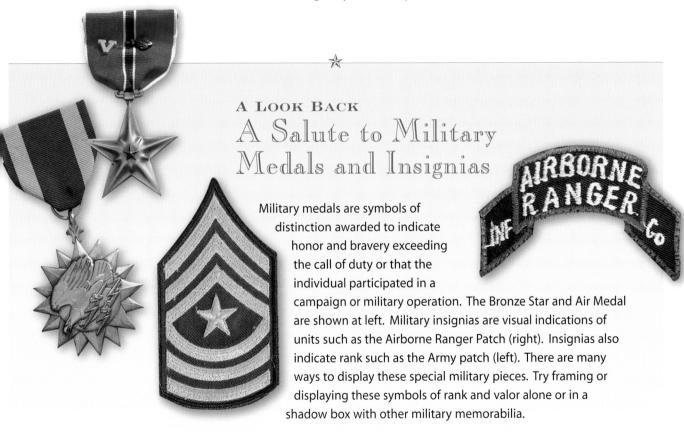

A LOOK BACK
A Salute to Military Medals and Insignias

Military medals are symbols of distinction awarded to indicate honor and bravery exceeding the call of duty or that the individual participated in a campaign or military operation. The Bronze Star and Air Medal are shown at left. Military insignias are visual indications of units such as the Airborne Ranger Patch (right). Insignias also indicate rank such as the Army patch (left). There are many ways to display these special military pieces. Try framing or displaying these symbols of rank and valor alone or in a shadow box with other military memorabilia.

STRIPED STAR PILLOW

★

**THIS HANDSOME STAR PILLOW MAKES A BOLD PATRIOTIC STATEMENT.
ADORNED WITH RIBBON AND STAR APPLIQUÉS, THIS STRIKING ACCENT
PIECE CAN MAKE ITS HOME IN A DEN, LIVING ROOM, BEDROOM, OR PORCH.**

WHAT YOU'LL NEED

- ★ ⅝ yard of 60-inch-wide blue wool coating fabric
- ★ ⅛ yard of 60-inch-wide red wool coating fabric
- ★ 1 yard of ⅞-inch-wide novelty stripe grosgrain ribbon
- ★ Pinking shears or pinking edge rotary blade cutter
- ★ Hi-loft batting and poly-fil for inside star shape
- ★ 2 red star 2¼ inch appliqués
- ★ 2 red star 1¼ inch appliqués
- ★ 4 blue star 1¼ inch appliqués
- ★ Fabric glue

Note: The star shape includes a ⅜-inch seam.

HERE'S HOW

1 Enlarge and trace pattern, *below*. Rotating the pattern to make a star shape. From blue wool, cut two stars for front and back and a 3¼×60-inch strip for boxing. From red wool, cut 1½×36–inch pinked edge strip. Cut the red strip in half. Refer to the photograph, *opposite,* and place the red wool on the star. Center stripe ribbon on the red wool and top stitch along the edge of the ribbon.

2 Layer the boxing strip on the pillow front, wrong sides together. Stitch the seam, clipping boxing strip around points as necessary. Stitch the boxing strip to the pillow back.

3 Make a 5-inch slit in star back. Pink edges through both layers. Cut two layers of high-loft batting into a star shape. Stuff one batting layer through the opening. Add poly-fil to the desired firmness. Stuff the remaining batting in the pillow. Hand-stitch the opening closed. Glue star appliqués on the pillow front.

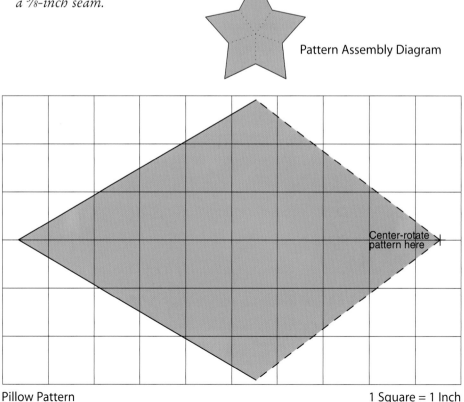

Pattern Assembly Diagram

Pillow Pattern

Center-rotate pattern here

1 Square = 1 Inch

RED, WHITE, AND BLUE

FROM YOUR
KITCHEN

PATRIOTIC SALAD

HURRAH FOR THE RED, WHITE, AND BLUE! THIS CELEBRATION-STYLE SALAD IS THE PERFECT DISH TO TAKE TO A POTLUCK.

WHAT YOU'LL NEED

★ *1 6-ounce package strawberry-flavored gelatin*
★ *1 10-ounce package frozen strawberries*
★ *1 8-ounce package cream cheese, softened*
★ *1 8-ounce carton dairy sour cream*
★ *¾ cup salad dressing or mayonnaise*
★ *1 tablespoon lemon juice*
★ *1 envelope unflavored gelatin*
★ *1 6-ounce package blackberry-flavored gelatin*
★ *2 cups frozen blueberries*

Add another layer at the stage when the gelatin retains a fingerprint.

HERE'S HOW

1 Lightly oil an 11- to 12-cup mold; set aside.

2 Pour 2 cups boiling water over the strawberry-flavored gelatin; stir until the gelatin is dissolved. Carefully stir in the frozen strawberries. Chill until the mixture beings to thicken. To quick-chill gelatin, place the bowl of gelatin over a bowl of ice water; stir until partially set. Stir to evenly distribute the strawberries and turn the mixture into the prepared mold. Refrigerate.

3 In a small bowl beat cream cheese, sour cream, salad dressing or mayonnaise, and lemon juice until the mixture is smooth.

4 In a small custard cup sprinkle the unflavored gelatin into ¼ cup cold water. Place the custard cup in a skillet with ½ inch of boiling water. Stir the gelatin until dissolved. Stir the unflavored gelatin mixture into the cream cheese mixture. Beat until well blended. Carefully spoon the gelatin-cream cheese mixture over the strawberry mixture. Spread the gelatin-cream cheese mixture evenly to the edge of the mold. Refrigerate.

5 Pour 2 cups boiling water over the blackberry-flavored gelatin and stir until the gelatin is dissolved. Add ½ cup cold water and the blueberries; stir. Chill until the mixture begins to thicken. Stir again to distribute the blueberries. Spoon the mixture over the cream cheese layer in the mold and spread evenly to the edge of the mold.

6 Refrigerate the gelatin mold until it is firm, overnight or several hours. Unmold onto a serving dish.

7 To unmold gelatin, loosen the edges of the mixture from the sides of the mold with the tip of a sharp knife or thin metal spatula. Set the mold in warm (not hot) water to the depth of the gelatin contents. Hold about 5 seconds. Tilt or shake the mold gently to loosen. Invert the serving plate on top of the mold. Hold both together firmly and invert. Shake the mold gently until the gelatin slips from the mold onto the serving dish or plate. If the gelatin doesn't release, repeat the process. Makes 12 servings.

Tip From Our Kitchen

★ For a successful layered gelatin salad, add the second layer when the first layer appears firm but is slightly sticky to the touch. At this stage the gelatin will retain a fingerprint, as shown at *left*. If the first layer is chilled too long, the second layer won't adhere; if it's not chilled long enough, the layers run together.

TOMATO-PEACH BBQ RIBS

AS A SURPRISING CHANGE FROM TRADITIONAL BARBECUE SAUCE,
PEACHES, TOMATO SOUP, AND OTHER FLAVORINGS COMBINE IN A
NOT-TOO-SWEET COATING FOR SUCCULENT PORK RIBS.

WHAT YOU'LL NEED

- ★ 4 to 5 pounds pork ribs, cut into serving-size pieces
- ★ 1 onion studded with 2 whole cloves
- ★ 1 bay leaf
- ★ 2 cups chopped, peeled peaches (1 pound)
- ★ 1 10¾-ounce can condensed tomato soup
- ★ ½ cup light corn syrup
- ★ ½ cup cider vinegar
- ★ ½ cup packed brown sugar
- ★ ¼ cup cooking oil
- ★ 1 tablespoon dry mustard
- ★ 1 tablespoon Worcestershire sauce
- ★ 1½ teaspoons paprika
- ★ ½ teaspoon salt
- ★ ½ teaspoon garlic powder
- ★ ½ teaspoon black pepper

HERE'S HOW

1 Place the ribs in a 5-quart Dutch oven and add about 2 inches of water. Add the onion and bay leaf and bring the water to a boil. Reduce heat; cover and simmer about 1 hour or until the ribs are tender.

2 Drain the ribs. In a covered grill arrange medium-hot coals around a drip pan. Test for medium heat above the pan by holding hand over coals for 4 seconds. Place the ribs, fat side up, on the preheated grill rack over the drip pan, but not over the coals. Lower the grill hood and cook for 1 hour.

3 Meanwhile, in a 2-quart saucepan stir together the peaches, tomato soup, corn syrup, vinegar, brown sugar, cooking oil, dry mustard, Worcestershire sauce, paprika, salt, garlic powder, and pepper. Bring the mixture to a boil, stirring constantly. Reduce heat and simmer, uncovered, about 20 minutes or until the sauce is slightly thickened, stirring occasionally.

4 After the ribs have grilled for 1 hour, brush them generously with the sauces. Grill for 5 to 10 minutes more or until well-done, brushing occasionally with the sauce. Pass the remaining sauce with the ribs. Makes 6 servings.

Tips From Our Kitchen

- ★ Leftover sauce can be stored in the refrigerator for 2 weeks to use on pork chops, chicken, or other poultry. To use, heat the sauce to boiling and brush it on the almost-cooked meat during the last 5 to 20 minutes of cooking.
- ★ Two cups frozen, unsweetened peach slices that have been thawed and chopped can be substituted for the fresh peaches in this recipe.
- ★ To grill ribs without precooking them, follow Step 2, except use medium coals and grill the ribs for 2 hours. To roast the ribs instead of grilling, place them fat side up in shallow roasting pan. Bake in a 350°F oven about 2 hours or until well-done. Brush on the sauce during the last 5 to 10 minutes.

UPPER LEFT: *Use your choice of pork ribs: spareribs, country-style ribs, or back ribs.*

LOWER LEFT: *Cut the pork into serving-size pieces before cooking.*

PICNIC-PERFECT CHICKEN

COUNTRY MEETS CITY IN THIS BARBECUE SAUCE THAT'S PERFECT FOR
THE FOURTH OF JULY. SHERRY SUPPLIES THE UPTOWN FLAVOR.

WHAT YOU'LL NEED

- ★ *3 to 4 pounds meaty chicken pieces (breasts, thighs, and drumsticks)*
- ★ *1½ cups dry sherry*
- ★ *1 cup finely chopped onion*
- ★ *¼ cup lemon juice*
- ★ *6 cloves garlic, minced*
- ★ *2 bay leaves*
- ★ *1 15-ounce can tomato puree*
- ★ *¼ cup honey*
- ★ *3 tablespoons molasses*
- ★ *1 teaspoon salt*
- ★ *½ teaspoon dried thyme, crushed*
- ★ *¼ to ½ teaspoon ground red pepper*
- ★ *¼ teaspoon black pepper*
- ★ *2 tablespoons white vinegar*

HERE'S HOW

1 Place chicken in a self-sealing plastic bag set in a shallow dish. For marinade, in a medium bowl stir together sherry, onion, lemon juice, garlic, and bay leaves. Pour over chicken; seal bag. Marinate in the refrigerator for 2 to 4 hours, turning bag occasionally. Drain chicken, reserving marinade. Cover and chill chicken until ready to grill.

2 For sauce, in a large saucepan combine the reserved marinade, the tomato puree, honey, molasses, salt, thyme, red pepper, and black pepper. Bring to boiling; reduce heat. Simmer, uncovered, about 30 minutes or until reduced to 2 cups. Remove from heat; remove bay leaves. Stir in vinegar.

3 For a charcoal grill, arrange medium-hot coals around a drip pan. Test for medium heat above the pan by holding hand over coals for 4 seconds. Place chicken pieces, bone sides down, on grill rack over drip pan. Cover and grill for 50 to 60 minutes or until tender and no longer pink, brushing with some of the sauce during the last 15 minutes of grilling. (For a gas grill, preheat grill. Reduce heat to medium. Adjust for indirect cooking. Grill as above.) To serve, reheat and pass the remaining sauce with chicken. Makes 6 servings.

SKILLET POTATO SALAD

THIS COOKED-IN-THE-SKILLET POTATO SALAD IS THE PERFECT ALL-AMERICAN SIDE DISH.

WHAT YOU'LL NEED

★ *1 pound potatoes, cut into 1-inch pieces (do not peel potatoes)*
★ *2 tablespoons cooking oil or olive oil*
★ *$^1/_4$ teaspoon salt*
★ *$^1/_8$ teaspoon black pepper*
★ *2 medium summer squash, cut into 1$^1/_2$-inch pieces (8 ounces total)*
★ *$^1/_3$ cup bottled Italian vinaigrette or other oil-and-vinegar salad dressing*
★ *1 small red sweet pepper, cut into $^1/_2$- to $^3/_4$-inch squares*
★ *6 cherry tomatoes, halved*
★ *$^1/_4$ cup snipped fresh parsley*
★ *1 teaspoon snipped fresh thyme*
★ *Sprigs of fresh thyme (optional)*

HERE'S HOW

1 In a large skillet cook potatoes in hot oil over medium heat about 15 minutes or until tender and brown on all sides, turning occasionally. Spoon potatoes into a serving bowl. Sprinkle with the salt and pepper.

2 To same skillet add summer squash. Cook and stir over medium heat for 3 to 5 minutes or until just tender. Add to the potatoes in the serving bowl.

3 Pour dressing over potatoes and summer squash. Add sweet pepper, tomatoes, parsley, and thyme. Toss gently to mix. Cool.

4 Cover and chill for 4 to 24 hours, stirring salad occasionally. Top with thyme sprigs, if desired. Makes 6 side-dish servings.

WATERMELON WITH SALSA

★

WHAT COULD BE MORE RED THAN COOL, CRISP WATERMELON WITH
A DASH OF SPICY SALSA? THIS UNEXPECTED COMBINATION WILL BE A
WELCOME TREAT AT YOUR NEXT SUMMER GET-TOGETHER.

WHAT YOU'LL NEED

*★ 2 cups melon, such as
cantaloupe, honeydew, or seedless
yellow or red watermelon, cut
into ¼- to ½-inch cubes
★ ¼ cup bottled sangria or
sparkling white grape juice
★ 2 tablespoons finely chopped
fresh jalapeño pepper, seeds
removed (optional)
★ 4 2-inch-thick slices cut from
half of a seedless red watermelon,
chilled and halved
★ 1 tablespoon lemon juice*

HERE'S HOW

1 For salsa, in a medium bowl combine cubed melon, sangria or grape juice, and, if desired, jalapeño pepper. Toss gently. Cover and chill for 2 to 6 hours.
2 Place 2 chilled watermelon "steaks" on each serving plate. Sprinkle with lemon juice. Spoon some of the salsa over each serving. Makes 4 servings.

PASS-THE-PEAS SALAD

WATERMELON WITH SALSA

THREE-CHEERS BEAN SALAD

PASS-THE-PEAS SALAD

FRESH PEA PODS ADD PIZZAZZ TO THIS MOSTLY WHITE MACARONI SALAD.

WHAT YOU'LL NEED

* ★ 1 cup fresh pea pods
* ★ 8 ounces dried elbow macaroni
* ★ 1 cup frozen peas, thawed
* ★ 1/2 cup mayonnaise or salad dressing
* ★ 1/2 cup dairy sour cream
* ★ 1/3 cup milk
* ★ 1/4 cup horseradish mustard
* ★ 2 cloves garlic, minced
* ★ 1/4 teaspoon salt
* ★ 1/4 teaspoon black pepper
* ★ 3/4 cup thinly sliced celery
* ★ 2 tablespoons chopped onion
* ★ Milk (optional)
* ★ Pea pods (optional)

HERE'S HOW

1 Remove tips and strings from pea pods. Cook macaroni according to package directions in lightly salted boiling water, adding pea pods and peas during last 1 minute of cooking. Drain and rinse. Halve pea pods diagonally; set pasta and pea pods aside.

2 In a small bowl stir together mayonnaise, sour cream, milk, mustard, minced garlic, salt, and pepper; set aside.

3 In a large bowl combine the cooked macaroni and pea mixture, celery, and onion. Pour mayonnaise mixture over macaroni mixture. Stir gently to combine.

4 Cover; chill 4 to 24 hours. Stir mixture before serving. If desired, add milk (1 to 2 tablespoons) to moisten. Top with additional pea pods, if desired. Makes 12 to 16 side-dish servings.

THREE-CHEERS BEAN SALAD

SERVED IN A BRIGHT BLUE DISH, BEANS TEAM UP FOR A TASTY TRIO.

WHAT YOU'LL NEED

* ★ 2/3 cup cider vinegar
* ★ 1/4 cup salad oil
* ★ 1 tablespoon dark brown sugar
* ★ 1/2 teaspoon salt
* ★ 1/4 teaspoon black pepper
* ★ 1 15-ounce can garbanzo beans, rinsed and drained
* ★ 1 15-ounce can small white beans, rinsed and drained
* ★ 1 10-ounce package frozen lima beans, thawed
* ★ 2 medium carrots, thinly bias-sliced (1 cup)
* ★ 2 small fresh jalapeño or serrano peppers, seeded and finely chopped
* ★ 1/3 cup snipped fresh cilantro

HERE'S HOW

1 For dressing, in a small bowl whisk together the vinegar, oil, brown sugar, salt, and pepper; set aside.

2 In a large self-sealing plastic bag set in a deep bowl combine garbanzo beans, white beans, lima beans, carrots, peppers, and cilantro. Pour dressing over bean mixture. Close bag. Marinate in the refrigerator for 2 to 24 hours, turning bag occasionally.

3 Transfer to a serving bowl. Makes 8 servings.

Use any of these optional ingredients in the bean salad:
* ★ Lime wedges
* ★ Kosher salt, sea salt, or other coarse-grained or regular salt
* ★ Bottled hot pepper sauce
* ★ Sprigs of fresh cilantro

RED, WHITE & BLUE TART

WAVE YOUR FLAGS, TOOT YOUR HORNS, AND JOIN IN THE PARADE!
IT'S TIME TO CHEER FOR THIS STARRY TART THAT QUICKLY LIBERATES
YOU FROM THE KITCHEN.

WHAT YOU'LL NEED

- ★ *1 20-ounce roll refrigerated sugar cookie dough*
- ★ *Coarse sugar*
- ★ *1 14-ounce can (1¼ cups) sweetened condensed milk or fat-free sweetened condensed milk*
- ★ *½ cup dairy sour cream or light dairy sour cream*
- ★ *½ teaspoon finely shredded lemon or lime peel*
- ★ *⅓ cup lemon or lime juice*
- ★ *1 cup fresh blueberries or blackberries*
- ★ *2 cups fresh red raspberries or 3 cups fresh strawberry halves*

HERE'S HOW

1 Preheat oven to 375°F. For crust, generously grease the bottom of an 11×8×1½-inch rectangular tart pan with a removable bottom or an 11- to 12-inch pizza pan; lightly grease sides. With floured hands, pat half of the dough onto bottom and up the sides of the pan.

2 For cookies, on a lightly floured surface roll out the remaining half of the dough to ⅛- to ¼-inch thickness. Using small star cutters, cut into shapes. Place cutouts on an ungreased baking sheet. Reroll trimmings and cut. Sprinkle half with coarse sugar.

3 Bake crust and cookies until golden, allowing 4 to 5 minutes for small cookies and 12 minutes for crust. Cool on a wire rack.

4 For filling, in a mixing bowl combine condensed milk, sour cream, lemon or lime peel, and juice. Stir about 3 minutes or until mixture is thickened. Cover and chill until ready to assemble tart.

5 To assemble tart, loosen and remove sides of pan from crust, if desired. Transfer crust to a platter, leaving bottom of pan under crust. Before serving, spread filling onto crust. Top with berries and cookies. Cut into squares. Makes 12 servings.

Decorate cookies that don't fit on the tart with canned frosting tinted red or blue.

LEMONADE MOUSSE

GARNISHED WITH BLUEBERRIES AND STRAWBERRIES OR RASPBERRIES IN HONOR OF AMERICA, THIS LIGHT DESSERT IS A GRAND FINALE TO ANY GET-TOGETHER.

WHAT YOU'LL NEED

- *1 envelope unflavored gelatin*
- *⅓ cup sugar*
- *1 cup water*
- *⅔ cup frozen lemonade concentrate, thawed*
- *4 drops red food coloring*
- *1 cup whipping cream*
- *½ cup fresh blueberries*
- *3 thin lemon slices, halved, or pink grapefruit half slices (optional)*
- *Lemon peel curls (optional)*

HERE'S HOW

1 In a small saucepan combine gelatin and sugar; add ⅔ cup of the water. Cook and stir over medium heat until dissolved. Remove from heat. Stir in remaining water and lemonade concentrate. Divide mixture in half, and transfer each half to a medium bowl. Stir red food coloring into one portion of the mixture. Cover and chill both mixtures about 1¼ to 1½ hours or until mixtures mound.

2 In a chilled bowl beat whipping cream with an electric mixer on medium speed until soft peaks form (tips curl); set aside.

3 Wash beaters. Beat plain mixture with electric mixer on medium speed about 30 seconds or until light and foamy. Beat pink mixture until light and foamy. Fold half the whipped cream into each lemonade mixture.

4 Carefully layer plain mixture and pink mixture into 6 small serving glasses or dessert dishes, dividing evenly.

5 Cover and chill at least 2 hours before serving. Garnish with berries, and, if desired, citrus slices and lemon peel curls. Makes 6 servings.

RALLY 'ROUND THE FLAG

*

GIFTS TO CHERISH FOREVER

CANDY FOR THE KIDS

LAYER THE COLORS OF INDEPENDENCE DAY IN MILK BOTTLES FOR A FUN AND FESTIVE GIFT. THESE HOLIDAY TREATS ARE READY TO SHARE—AND THEY STORE EASILY BY COVERING WITH PLASTIC WRAP AND SECURING WITH COLORFUL RUBBER BANDS.

WHAT YOU'LL NEED
★ *Milk bottles (available in antiques stores and flea markets)*
★ *Candies in red, white, and blue*
★ *Plastic wrap*
★ *Rubber bands in red, white, and blue*

HERE'S HOW
1 Wash the milk bottles. Let the bottles dry.
2 Fill the bottles with red, white, and blue candies. To store food in bottles, cover the top with plastic wrap and secure it with a brightly colored rubber band.

STAR-RIMMED BASKET

★

THE PERFECT PRESENT FOR EVERY PATRIOT, THIS
WHITEWASHED BASKET IS TRIMMED WITH PRECUT WOOD STARS THAT
ARE PAINTED RED AND BLUE.

WHAT YOU'LL NEED

- ★ Basket
- ★ White gel stain
- ★ Disposable foam plates
- ★ Paintbrush
- ★ Acrylic paints in barn red and navy
- ★ Wood stars 1 to 2½ inches wide
- ★ Fine-grit sandpaper
- ★ Tack cloth
- ★ Hot-glue gun; hotmelt adhesive

HERE'S HOW

1 Place some gel stain on a foam plate. Paint the basket using gel stain and wide flat paintbrush, using vertical strokes to cover well. Let the stain dry. For opaque coverage, apply a second coat.
2 Put a dab of barn red and a dab if navy blue paint on a foam plate. Thin each paint with water, about one part paint to one part water. Paint the stars. Let the paint dry.
3 Using fine-grit sandpaper, lightly sand the edges of the painted stars to create a worn look. Brush off dust and wipe with a tack cloth.
4 Layer and glue contrasting small stars on large stars. Glue the stars onto the basket rim, alternating star colors and sizes.

STARRY BUBBLE WANDS

AIRY BUBBLES WILL FLOAT ON EVERY BREEZE WITH THESE STAR-SHAPE BUBBLE WANDS—A PERFECT GIFT FOR ANY AGE.

WHAT YOU'LL NEED

* ★ *Medium size star-shape cookie cutter*
* ★ *40-inch piece of 20-gauge wire*
* ★ *Wire cutters*
* ★ *Electric drill*
* ★ *Spray paint in desired color*

HERE'S HOW

1 Fold a 40-inch piece of wire in half. Starting at one point of the star, bend the wire around the cookie cutter to outline star. When the wire meets, twist to secure.

2 Straighten the ends of the wire and trim them with wire cutters to an even length. Insert the trimmed ends into the chuck on an electric drill and tighten the chuck. Hold the wire taut and rotate the drill until the wire is twisted to the desired tightness. Loosen the chuck and remove the wire. Trim the ends again.

3 Carefully remove the star from the cookie cutter. Spray-paint the star. Let the paint dry.

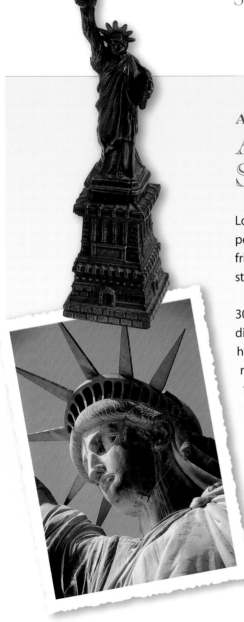

A LOOK BACK
A Salute to the Statue of Liberty

Located in New York Harbor, the Statue of Liberty was a gift from the people of France to the people of the United States in recognition of the friendship established during the American Revolution. Today the Statue stands as a universal symbol of political freedom and democracy.

Made of copper, steel, and concrete, the Statue soars more than 300 feet high. Visitors climb the 22 stories to reach the crown that displays 25 windows that symbolize the earth's gemstones and the heaven's rays shining over the world. The seven rays of the crown represent the seven seas and continents of the world. The tablet that the Statue holds in her left hand is inscribed "July 4th, 1776."

The United States financed and designed the Statue pedestal. In France, sculptor Frederic Auguste Bartholdi and designer Alexandre Gustave Eiffel worked together to design the Statue. When completed, it was shipped in 350 pieces and reassembled on the pedestal.

On October 28, 1886, after four months of construction, President Grover Cleveland accepted the Statue on behalf of the United States and said in part: "We will not forget that Liberty has here made her home; nor shall her chosen altar be neglected."

The Statue of Liberty was designated as a National Monument in 1924.

PICNIC BASKET COVER

PICNIC LOVERS WILL BE THRILLED TO RECEIVE THIS STRIKING BASKET COVER USING QUILT BLOCKS IN ALL-AMERICAN COLORS.

TIP BEFORE STARTING

Measure picnic basket lid to determine what size to cut fabrics. This cover is designed to fit a basket lid that measures 13×20 inches. Make measurement adjustments for your picnic basket cover before beginning the project. Seam allowances are ¼-inch wide.

WHAT YOU'LL NEED

★ *Two 9½ inch Woven Star blocks in coordinating colors*
★ *1¾ yards of red check fabric*
★ *¼ yard of white fabric*
★ *2 yards of piping cord*
★ *15×22-inch piece of fleece*
★ *15×22-inch piece of backing fabric*
★ *2—2½-inch star appliqués*

CUTTING THE FABRIC

To make the best use of fabrics, cut pieces in the following order.

From red check fabric, cut:
★ *1—36-inch square. From the square, cut enough 5½-inch bias strips to piece two 55-inch strips for ties and two 45-inch ruffle strips*
★ *1—13-inch square. From the square, cut enough 1½-inch bias strips to piece two 40-inch cording strips*
★ *2—10½×13½-inch backing pieces*
★ *4—2½×9½-inch sashing strips*
★ *2—1½×13½-inch sashing strips*

From white fabric, cut:
★ *2—3½×42-inch strips for ruffle*

HERE'S HOW

1 **MAKE THE COVER TOP:** Make two blocks, following the instructions on *page 54* for each block. Sew the two blocks together. Beginning at one outer edge of a quilt block, sew a 2½×9½-inch red check sashing strip. Stop stitching ¼ inch from inner edge of block. Repeat with three remaining sashing strips, sewing to the top and bottom of two blocks, leaving an opening. Sew a 1½×13½-inch sashing strip to each side of the cover. Layer pieced top and fleece together; baste. Quilt as desired. Trim fleece to match the top. Cut a slit in the fleece 2½-inches long at center top and bottom for a vent.

2 **ASSEMBLE THE BASKET LID COVER:** Cut two pieces of piping cord, each 36 inches long. Cover the piping cord with the 1½-inch bias strips. Position one piping cord on one side of the cover front, raw edges together, beginning and ending at the vent opening. Stitch the piping to the top. Stitch the second piping cord to the top. Trim raw edges to match the cover edges. Right sides together, join one red check 5½×45-inch bias strip with one white 3½×42-inch strip lengthwise to make a 8½×42-inch ruffle strip. Repeat for a second ruffle strip. With right sides together, fold ends of ruffle in half lengthwise. Sew across ruffle ends. Turn to right side; press. Position finished edges of ruffle ¼ inch from edge of vent. Gather raw edges, adjusting around one half of the top. Stitch ruffle over piping, matching raw edges. Sew ruffle to second half of basket top. Measure 2½ inches from each top and bottom edge of 10½×13½-inch backing squares. Sew together, beginning and ending at the 2½ inch mark. Lay cover back on cover top, right sides together. Begin ¼ inch from a vent and sew to opposite side, stopping ¼ inch from vent. Repeat for the second backing square, leaving an opening for turning along a side seam. Stitch. Trim corners; turn right side out. Stitch opening closed. Turn under seam allowances on sashing and back at vent; turn to back side of cover. Hand-stitch facing hem.

3 **FINISHING THE BASKET LID COVER:** With right sides together, sew each tie together lengthwise, tapering to a point on both ends, and leaving an opening for turning. Trim corners. Turn to right side. Stitch openings closed; press. Make a pleat at the center of each tie. Stitch each tie over a vent opening. Glue or sew an appliquéd star to center of each block. Place cover on basket; tie a bow around handles.

pattern and instructions continued on page 54

Woven Star Quarter Block

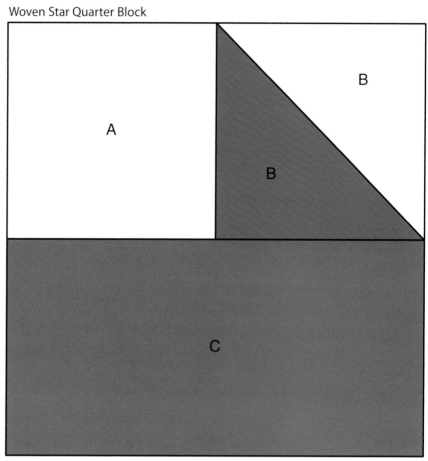

HOW TO CONSTRUCT THIS BLOCK

Make BB unit (8 times). Sew BB to A (8 times). Join BBA to C (8 times). Rotate and sew two BBAC's together (4 times) to make two blocks. Sew the two blocks together.

"Terrorists attacked a symbol of American prosperity. They did not touch its source. America is successful because of the hard work, and creativity, and enterprise of our people."

— GEORGE W. BUSH IN HIS ADDRESS TO THE CONGRESS AND AMERICAN PEOPLE, SEPT. 20, 2001

CELEBRATE PLATE

WRITE A MESSAGE FOR A SPECIAL OCCASION ON A CAKE PLATE, AND CELEBRATE IN STYLE.

WHAT YOU'LL NEED

- ★ *Tracing paper*
- ★ *Scissors*
- ★ *Clear glass cake plate*
- ★ *White vinegar*
- ★ *Tape*
- ★ *Paint pens in desired colors (usually used for fabric and available at art, crafts, and discount stores)*

HERE'S HOW

1 Trace around the outer edge of the plate onto tracing paper and cut out. Draw a smaller circle inside the paper pattern to indicate the plate rim. Write "CELEBRATE" or another message within the rim area indicated on the tracing paper.

2 Wash the plate with hot water and rinse with white vinegar to remove any fingerprints. Let the plate dry. Tape the paper pattern with the message on top of the plate, right side up. Turn the plate facedown. The message can be seen backward through the tracing paper. Use the paint pens to write on the underside of the plate, following the pencil lines on the pattern.

3 Allow the paint to dry several hours or overnight. Remove the pattern and turn the plate over. (*Note:* The back of the plate is not washable. To write a new message, simply peel the paint off the back of the plate.)

To: Be...
From:
Elizabeth

DYNAMIC DISHES

PAINTED POLKA DOTS AND STRIPES TRANSFORM PLAIN GLASS DISHES INTO GRAND DINNERWARE TO GIVE TO SPECIAL FRIENDS. NO PATTERNS ARE NEEDED—JUST BRUSH STROKES AND PENCIL DABS!

WHAT YOU'LL NEED

* ★ *Clear glass dishes*
* ★ *Glass paints in red, white, and blue*
* ★ *½-inch flat paintbrush*
* ★ *Pencil*

HERE'S HOW

1 Wash and dry the dishes. Avoid touching the areas to be painted.

2 For the plate, all painting is done on the back side of the plate. For the cup and bowl, all painting is done on the outside. Using the flat paintbrush, paint red checks around the rim of the plate and cup, leaving room for white. For the bowl, paint red stripes around the bowl, leaving ½ inch at the rim unpainted. Let dry. Paint white checks on the plate and cup. Paint stripes on the bowl. Let dry.

3 To make blue dots, dip the eraser end of a pencil into paint and dot onto surface. Let dry.

4 Bake and cool the glassware in the oven as instructed by the paint manufacturer. Hand-wash the dishes.

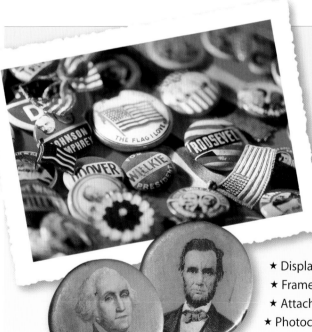

A LOOK BACK

A Salute to Political Pins

If you have a collection of patriotic pins, display them proudly. Here are some ways to display and use historical pins:

* ★ Attach to the front of a velvet pillow.
* ★ Pin to a fabric window valance.
* ★ Display in a collage with other presidential memorabilia.
* ★ Frame pins separately for a striking effect.
* ★ Attach magnets to the back and arrange on the refrigerator.
* ★ Photocopy pins to make original note paper.
* ★ Wear a cluster of pins on a denim jacket or on a wool scarf.
* ★ Pin to stuffed animals, such as teddy bears (named after Teddy Roosevelt).
* ★ Pin to a grapevine wreath or swag, and adorn the wreath with red, white, and blue ribbons.

If you're new to collecting political pins, start by purchasing one pin at a time. Splurge on a vintage pin occasionally and display your rare finds among current, less expensive pins.

SHOW YOUR COLORS

✦

FEEL
PROUD

WOVEN COLORS VEST

WOVEN TOGETHER LIKE THE UNITED PEOPLE OF OUR COUNTRY, THIS RIBBON-EMBELLISHED VEST SINGS OF THE RED, WHITE, AND BLUE.

WHAT YOU'LL NEED

★ *Vest pattern, such as KWIK SEW No. 2209, size medium, view C*
★ *Red wool fabric and lining according to pattern*
★ *Foam core board*
★ *Straight pins*
★ *2½ yards each of three different blue ribbons in widths ½ to ⅞ inch*
★ *2½ yards each of three different red ribbons in widths ½ to ⅞ inch*
★ *Notions according to pattern*
★ *Three ⅞-inch covered button kits*
★ *1½ yards light weight nonwoven fusible interfacing*
★ *Six ⅝-inch shank gold-color star buttons*

HERE'S HOW

1 For the woven lapel, work a 6×16-inch piece of ribbon weaving for one lapel. Repeat for opposite lapel, reversing ribbon colors. Trace the lapel pattern onto fusible side of interfacing, allowing several inches past the shape. Pin interfacing to foam core board, fusible side up.

2 Starting at the top inside corner of the pattern, pin a ribbon on the bias to corner (45 degree angle). Continue pinning ribbons to cover pattern area as shown in Diagram 1, *below*. Weave ribbons, pinning ends to foam core board as shown in Diagrams 2 and 3. With a warm iron and a press cloth, fuse ribbons to interfacing. Place and pin the pattern on ribbon weaving. Machine-stitch along edge of pattern. Cut out lapel just beyond stitching. Make opposite lapel by reversing the weaving pattern.

3 Cut and stitch vest according to pattern, featuring the welts and lapel binding in wool fabric. Cover buttons according to manufacturer's directions. Add three star buttons to each welt.

Ribbon Weaving Diagrams

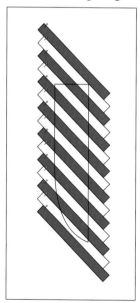  

Diagram 1   Diagram 2   Diagram 3

Woven Ribbon Detail

STITCHES & STRIPES MITTENS

THE COLORS OF OLD GLORY SHINE ON THESE TOASTY WARM
MITTENS. RIBBON STRIPES ACCENTED WITH FANCIFUL EMBROIDERY
STITCHES MAKE THIS PAIR OF MITTENS EXTRA SPECIAL.

WHAT YOU'LL NEED

★ *½ yard each of medium weight blue wool for mittens and light weight red wool for mitten lining*
★ *Scissors*
★ *1 yard each of six red or blue novelty ribbons in widths of ⅛, ⅜, ⅝, and ⅞ inch*
★ *No. 5 pearl cotton in shades of red, blue, and cream*
★ *Needle*
★ *Tracing paper*
★ *Pencil*
★ *1 yard of ¼-inch-wide elastic*
★ *½ yard of lining*
★ *¼ yard of red corduroy*

HERE'S HOW

1 For mitten hand back, cut two 13×6-inch pieces of blue wool. Arrange six ribbons lengthwise across mitten fabric, allowing space in between. Topstitch ribbons in place.

2 Work embroidery stitches as shown on *page 65*. For symmetrical pieces, work embroidery on one set of ribbons according to chart; reverse embroidery on the second piece.

3 Enlarge and trace the pattern pieces, *page 64*, onto tracing paper; cut out. Cut two sets of mitten pieces from wool and from lining (reversing for the opposite mitten).

4 Stitch all seams with right sides facing and using a ¼-inch seam allowance. Stitch the thumb to the thumb gusset around the curved edge from A to B. Stitch the inner seam of thumb and palm, tapering to a point at A. Machine-zigzag over the elastic stretched on the wrong side of the palm/thumb, 3 inches from the top edge. Stitch mitten palm to back along side and finger curve. Turn right side out. Repeat for the lining, leaving an opening for tuning in the side seam of the lining.

5 Cut two cuffs from corduroy, each 6½×12½ inches. Stitch the short ends of each cuff together. Press the seams open. Fold the cuff in half, wrong sides facing, and matching the raw edges.

6 Machine stitch along the folded edge of the mitten cuff. Ease-stitch along the top edge of the cuff and baste to the mitten.

7 Slip the mitten into the lining, matching the side seams and the thumb. Stitch around the top edge. Slip-stitch the opening in the lining closed. Tuck the lining into the mitten and turn down the cuff.

patterns and diagrams on pages 64–65

"America is best described by one word — freedom."

— DWIGHT D. EISENHOWER IN HIS MESSAGE TO CONGRESS, JANUARY 9, 1958

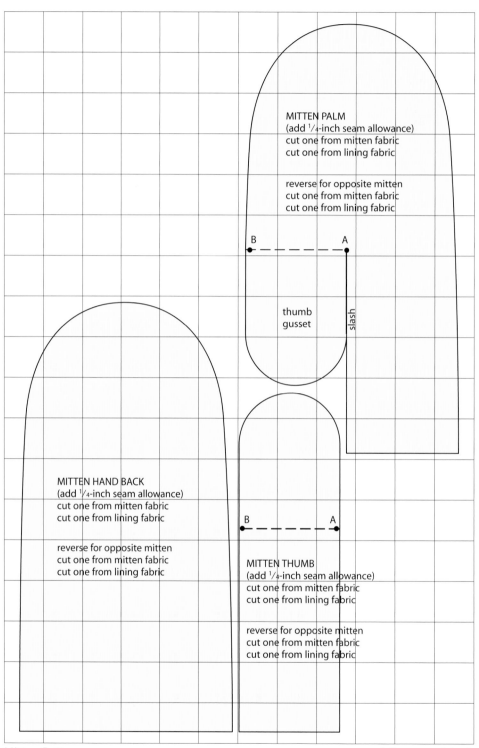

MITTEN PALM
(add ¼-inch seam allowance)
cut one from mitten fabric
cut one from lining fabric

reverse for opposite mitten
cut one from mitten fabric
cut one from lining fabric

B ● --------------- ● A

thumb
gusset

slash

MITTEN HAND BACK
(add ¼-inch seam allowance)
cut one from mitten fabric
cut one from lining fabric

reverse for opposite mitten
cut one from mitten fabric
cut one from lining fabric

B ● --------------- ● A

MITTEN THUMB
(add ¼-inch seam allowance)
cut one from mitten fabric
cut one from lining fabric

reverse for opposite mitten
cut one from mitten fabric
cut one from lining fabric

Mitten Patterns

1 Square = 1 Inch

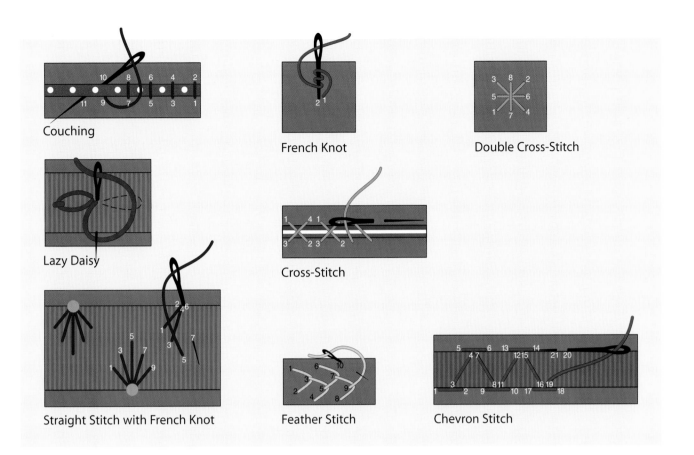

Couching

French Knot

Double Cross-Stitch

Lazy Daisy

Cross-Stitch

Straight Stitch with French Knot

Feather Stitch

Chevron Stitch

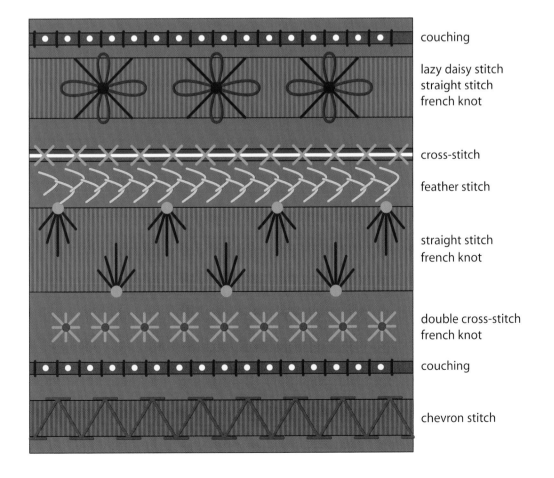

couching

lazy daisy stitch
straight stitch
french knot

cross-stitch

feather stitch

straight stitch
french knot

double cross-stitch
french knot

couching

chevron stitch

ALL-AMERICAN SWEATSHIRTS

★

SHOW LOVE FOR YOUR COUNTRY BY WEARING COLORS AND
SYMBOLS THAT SHOUT "AMERICA." THESE MOTHER AND DAUGHTER
DESIGNS CAN EASILY BE ADAPTED TO ANY SIZE SHIRT.

WHAT YOU'LL NEED

- ★ *Tracing paper*
- ★ *Pencil*
- ★ *Scissors*
- ★ *Sweatshirt in white or blue*
- ★ *Print fabrics in red and blue*
- ★ *½ yard fusible web*
- ★ *Gold and iridescent blue embroidery thread*
- ★ *Needle*
- ★ *Four 1-inch gold star sew-on emblems*
- ★ *½-inch gold shank button*
- ★ *1½-inch tassels on loops each in red, white, and blue*
- ★ *2-inch gold tassel on loop*

HERE'S HOW

1 Trace the star or heart pattern, *pages 68–69.* Cut out the pattern.
2 Measure the sweatshirt front to find the vertical center. Place pins to mark the center. To make the patterns for the stripes on the stars and stripes sweatshirt, cut three 2½×16-inch pieces from tracing paper. Pin the patterns horizontally on the sweatshirt, left ends at the center 2½ inches between the pattern pieces. Trim the right ends of the pattern pieces at the side seam of the sweatshirt.
3 Following the manufacturer's directions, fuse the fusible webbing to the back of the fabrics. Trace around the patterns on the paper backing of the fusible webbing. Cut out. Remove paper backing and fuse to sweatshirt.
4 Using blanket stitches and gold thread, outline the heart and the stars. Use blanket stitches and iridescent blue thread to outline the stripes.
5 For the heart sweatshirt, sew three star emblems across the heart. Sew one star at the bottom of the heart. Sew a gold button in center of star and hang tassels from the button.

patterns on page 68

★

A LOOK BACK
A Salute to Those Who Help from Home

Throughout history, seamstresses have used sewing skills in support of their country as well as to honor loved ones at war. People put their hearts and souls into every stitch when they sewed items such as parachutes, tents, flags, blankets, and uniforms. Quilts were also a passion and necessity during war. In 1863, more than 1,200 quilts were issued in one month to Union soldiers; some were made specifically for the troops, while others were family quilts sacrificed for the cause.

Heart Pattern

"If we cannot end now
our differences, at least we can
help make the world safe
for diversity."

— John F. Kennedy, June 10, 1963

"The future doesn't belong to the faint-hearted. It belongs to the brave."

— RONALD REAGAN, FROM A SPEECH ON JANUARY 28, 1986, ABOUT THE CHALLENGER TRAGEDY

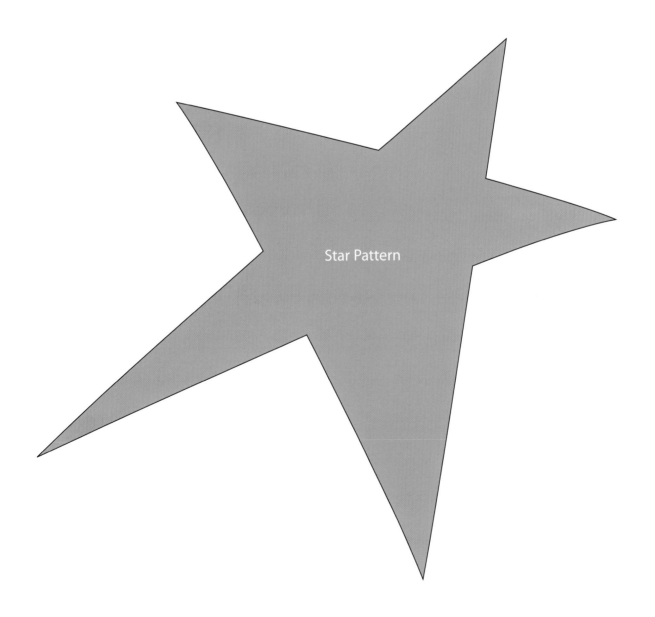

Star Pattern

CLEVER CAPS

★

HERE ARE THE PERFECT CAPS FOR ANY TIME YOU WANT TO SAY,
"I'M PROUD TO BE AN AMERICAN!" AND THESE TOPPERS ARE SO QUICK
AND EASY, THE KIDS CAN JOIN IN THE FUN.

WHAT YOU'LL NEED FOR THE WHITE HAT

★ *Red acrylic paint and brush*
★ *Decoupage medium*
★ *Red glitter*
★ *Gold glitter fabric paint*
★ *Assorted blue gems*

HERE'S HOW TO MAKE THE WHITE HAT

1 Paint bill of hat red. Let dry.
2 Coat thoroughly with decoupage medium. Cover well with red glitter. Shake off extra glitter.
3 Use gold glitter fabric paint to embellish the hat with a generous spot of paint. Press blue gems into the paint. Let the paint dry. Add lines, squiggles, or other desired designs. Let dry.

WHAT YOU'LL NEED FOR THE NAVY BLUE HAT

★ *Red chiffon scarf*
★ *Star shape buttons*
★ *Needle and thread*
★ *Strand of white beads*
★ *White ribbon*

HERE'S HOW TO MAKE THE NAVY BLUE HAT

1 Shape and twist a red chiffon scarf into a long strand with corners at opposite ends. Pull scarf through two gold star shape buttons.
2 Place scarf on hat, arranging buttons symmetrically on sides. From the inside, hand sew buttons to hat.
3 Wrap the scarf around the hat rim to the back. Slip both ends of the scarf into another button to hold in place.
4 Wind a strand of beads around red scarf. Tie strands of white ribbon in back around the star button. If desired, add more star buttons onto ends of red scarf.

LOYALTY RINGS

★

WITH SO MANY TYPES OF BEADS AVAILABLE, THERE'S NO LIMIT TO THESE PINKY PRETTIES. SIMPLY STRING YOUR FAVORITE BEADS ON ELASTIC THREAD TO MAKE RINGS FOR FLAG WAVERS OF ALL AGES.

WHAT YOU'LL NEED

★ *Elastic thread*
★ *Scissors*
★ *Small round and star beads in red, white, blue, silver, and gold*
★ *Small needle with large eye*

HERE'S HOW

1 Cut a 6-inch length of elastic thread. String on enough beads to make the desired size ring.

2 Thread one elastic end in needle. Push needle back through 5 or 6 beads. Clip thread and repeat with other end.

FLAG NECKLACE

★

**BEADED TO RESEMBLE THE STARS AND STRIPES,
THIS CLEVER NECKLACE IS A CHARMING ACCESSORY FOR
GIRLS OF ALL AGES.**

WHAT YOU'LL NEED

- ★ *Nine 1-inch-long head pins*
- ★ *Seed beads in red, white, and blue*
- ★ *Needlenose pliers*
- ★ *Metallic braid in red and silver*

HERE'S HOW

1 Thread 7 red and 6 white beads alternately onto four head pins. For each of the remaining 5 pins, thread 4 red and 3 white beads alternately onto the pin. Follow with 3 blue and 2 white, alternating beads.

2 Form the end of the pin into a circle with pliers.

3 Cut a 30-inch length of each color of metallic braid. Using the photo as a guide, thread beaded pins onto the braid. Knot at the sides of the beads. Knot again at the end of the necklace.

PRIDE PINS

FLAT GLASS MARBLES SERVE AS CANVASES FOR MINI MASTERPIECES. USING THE COLORS OF OUR FLAG, MAKING PRIDE PINS AS GIFTS IS AS EASY AS ONE-TWO-THREE!

WHAT YOU'LL NEED FOR THE GLASS MARBLE PINS

- ★ *Large flat glass marbles in blue, clear, red, or white*
- ★ *Glass paint in red, white, and blue*
- ★ *Paintbrush*
- ★ *Pin backs*
- ★ *Strong adhesive, such as E6000*

WHAT YOU'LL NEED FOR THE HORIZONTAL STARS PIN

- ★ *3 large and 3 small wood stars*
- ★ *Acrylic paint in red, white, and blue*
- ★ *Paintbrush; gold glitter paint*
- ★ *Hot-glue gun; hotmelt adhesive*
- ★ *Pin back; 8-inch piece of red, white, and blue ribbon*

WHAT YOU'LL NEED FOR THE CLUSTER STARS PIN

- ★ *3 small wood stars*
- ★ *Acrylic paint in red, white, and blue*
- ★ *Paintbrush*
- ★ *Silver glitter paint*
- ★ *Hot-glue gun; hotmelt adhesive*
- ★ *8-inch piece of red, white, and blue striped ribbon*
- ★ *Scissors*
- ★ *Pin back*

HERE'S HOW TO MAKE THE GLASS MARBLE PINS

1 Wash and dry the marbles. Avoid touching the area to be painted.
2 Using the photographs for ideas, paint hearts, stripes, dots, words, or other motifs on the rounded side of the marble. Allow paint to dry before layering colors. To make dots, use a pencil eraser for large dots, the handle of a paintbrush for medium dots, and a toothpick for small dots. Dip into paint and dot on surface. Let dry.
3 Apply a dot of adhesive to the pin back and place on the back of the marble near the top. Let the adhesive dry.

HERE'S HOW TO MAKE THE HORIZONTAL STARS PIN

1 Paint one large and one small star each color. Let dry. Paint a second coat, if desired. Let dry.
2 Paint the small stars and the edges of the large stars with glitter paint. Let dry.
3 Glue small stars on to large stars, using contrasting colors. Glue stars onto pin back. Let dry.
4 To wear, pin stars over a loop of ribbon.

HERE'S HOW TO MAKE THE CLUSTER STARS PIN

1 Paint stars red, white, and blue. Let dry. Paint a second coat, if desired. Let dry.
2 Paint each star with one coat of silver glitter paint. Let dry.
3 Measure ribbon and trim ends diagonally. Cross ribbon in the middle and glue to secure. Glue stars to ribbon. Let dry. Glue a pin back on the back of the ribbon. Let dry.

POSTAGE STAMP PINS

THE STAMPS THAT ONCE MOVED THE MAIL CAN NOW MOVE YOUR HEART. SIMPLY LAMINATE STAMPS TO SHOW YOUR SPIRIT. LOOPS OF RIBBON ADD OFFICIAL FLAIR.

WHAT YOU'LL NEED

★ *New or cancelled postage stamps*
★ *Straight scissors*
★ *Decorative edge scissors*
★ *Strong adhesive, such as E6000*
★ *Pin backs*

HERE'S HOW

1 Before beginning, refer to a postage stamp collector's book to make sure the stamps are not rare or valuable.

2 If the stamps have been used, carefully remove any paper backing. To remove, tear or cut off the upper right-hand corner of the envelope. Soak it, stamp side down, in warm water. Once the stamp falls away from the paper, let it soak for a few minutes more to remove any remaining glue. Pick up the stamp with tongs and dry it between paper towels. Place it under a heavy book for several hours. If the stamp will not peel away from the backing, trim around the stamp using decorative-edge scissors.

3 Take stamps to a photocopy shop and have them laminated. You can fit several on one sheet, leaving approximately 1 inch between stamps for trimming.

4 Cut the stamps apart if several are on one laminating sheet. Trim around each stamp using decorative edge scissors.

5 Glue a pin back to the back of the laminated stamp near the top. Let dry.

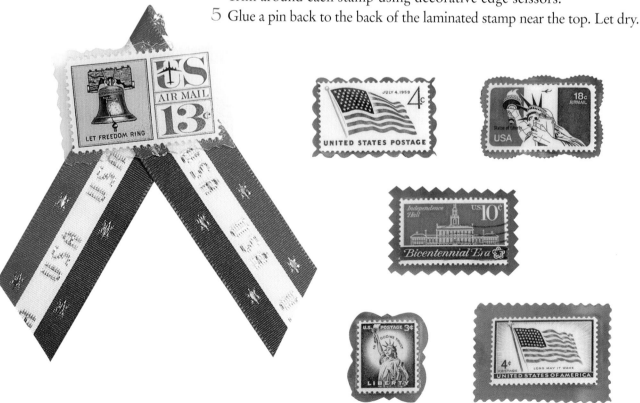

★74★

BEADED BEAUTY

★

**PLACE THIS GLISTENING PIN ON YOUR LAPEL TO SHOW
YOUR PATRIOTISM! THIS PRETTY PIN WORKS UP IN A JIFFY,
SO MAKE SEVERAL TO SHARE THE SPIRIT!**

WHAT YOU'LL NEED

★ *Large gem or button, or piece
from old jewelry*
★ *Small red, white, and blue
glass beads*
★ *Thin wire*
★ *Strong adhesive, such as E6000*
★ *White artist's tape*
★ *Pin back*

HERE'S HOW

1 Using a large gem for a base, glue another gem or decoration to the center with a small dot of adhesive.
2 String assorted beads on desired length of wire, allowing 2 inches of unbeaded wire at the ends. Loop the beaded wire and glue the wire ends onto the back of the gem.
3 Using white artist's tape, cover glued wire ends. Let dry.
4 Glue pin back onto back of gem. Let dry.

ALL-
AMERICAN
DESSERTS

*

AND,
OF COURSE,
APPLE PIE

RED, WHITE & BLUE PIE

THIS SATINY SMOOTH PIE, KISSED WITH PATRIOTIC COLORS, IS THE PERFECT FOIL FOR PLUMP, JUICY BERRIES OF EVERY KIND.

WHAT YOU'LL NEED

★ *1 recipe Pastry for Single-Crust Pie or 1/2 of a 15-ounce package refrigerated piecrust (1 crust)*
★ *1 6-ounce package (1 cup) semisweet chocolate pieces*
★ *1 tablespoon butter*
★ *1 8-ounce package cream cheese, softened*
★ *2 tablespoons orange liqueur*
★ *1/4 cup sifted powdered sugar*
★ *1 quart whole strawberries, rinsed and stems removed*
★ *1 cup mixed berries, such as blueberries and raspberries*
★ *2 tablespoons red currant jelly*
★ *1/2 cup whipping cream*
★ *2 tablespoons sifted powdered sugar*
★ *1/2 teaspoon finely shredded orange peel*

HERE'S HOW

1 Prepare and/or bake pastry shell; set aside. In a saucepan combine chocolate and butter. Heat and stir over medium-low heat until melted. Add cream cheese and liqueur. Heat and stir until combined. Remove from heat. Stir in the ¼ cup powdered sugar. Spread in baked pastry shell. Arrange strawberries and mixed berries on filling, placing strawberries stem ends down. Melt jelly; brush over berries. Cover; chill for 4 hours.

2 Let pie stand at room temperature for 30 minutes before serving. Beat whipping cream with the 2 tablespoons powdered sugar and the orange peel until soft peaks form. Spoon or pipe whipped cream into center of pie.

Pastry for Single-Crust Pie: Stir together 1¼ cups all-purpose flour and ¼ teaspoon salt. Using a pastry blender, cut in ⅓ cup shortening until pieces are pea-size. Sprinkle 1 tablespoon cold water over part of mixture; gently toss with a fork. Push moistened dough to side of bowl. Repeat, using 1 tablespoon of water at a time, until flour mixture is moistened (4 to 5 tablespoons total). Form dough into a ball. On a floured surface, roll dough into a 12-inch circle. Ease dough into a 9-inch pie plate. Trim to ½-inch beyond edge of plate. Fold under extra dough. Crimp edge. Prick bottom and sides of pastry. Line with a double thickness of foil. Bake in a 450°F oven 8 minutes. Remove foil. Bake 5 to 6 minutes more or until golden.

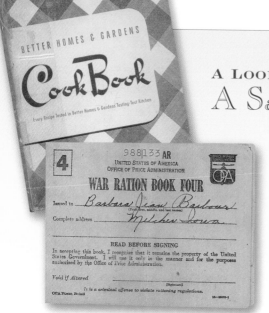

A LOOK BACK
A Salute to Special Recipes

During demanding times, cooks everywhere rose to the occasion by making recipes for their families that had to be altered because of lack of ingredients. Recipes without eggs, sugar, or other common ingredients were the norm as families adjusted to living without for the patriotic good. Pictured at *left* are the 1943 edition of the *Better Homes and Gardens*® *Cookbook* and a war ration book from World War II.

MARBLED STAR CUTOUTS

SIMPLY MARBLE-OUS! THESE CARDAMOM-LACED STAR CUTOUTS ARE A
COLORFUL ADDITION TO ANY COOKIE PLATTER.

WHAT YOU'LL NEED

- ★ ½ cup butter
- ★ 1 cup sugar
- ★ 1 teaspoon baking powder
- ★ 1 teaspoon finely shredded orange peel
- ★ ¼ teaspoon baking soda
- ★ ¼ teaspoon ground cardamom or ground nutmeg
- ★ ⅛ teaspoon salt
- ★ 1 egg
- ★ ½ cup dairy sour cream
- ★ 1 teaspoon vanilla
- ★ 2½ cups all-purpose flour
- ★ Assorted paste or liquid food coloring
- ★ Confectionary pearl sugar or colored sugar (optional)

HERE'S HOW

1 In a large mixing bowl beat butter with an electric mixer on medium to high speed for 30 seconds. Add sugar, baking powder, orange peel, baking soda, cardamom or nutmeg, and salt. Beat until combined. Beat in egg, sour cream, and vanilla. Beat in as much of the flour as you can with the mixer. Stir in remaining flour.

2 Divide dough in half. Wrap half of the dough in waxed paper or plastic wrap and refrigerate. Divide the remaining dough into 4 portions. Place each portion in a bowl. Add food coloring to each portion as desired, stirring until dough is evenly colored. Wrap each portion of dough in waxed paper or plastic wrap. Chill dough at least 2 hours or up to 24 hours.

3 On a lightly floured surface form a mound by dropping small amounts of each of the doughs close together in a random pattern (use half of the plain dough and half of each of the colored doughs). Shape the mound into a ball. Cover and refrigerate; repeat with remaining dough. On a lightly floured surface, roll 1 ball of dough to ⅛- to ¼-inch thickness. Using 2- to 3-inch cookie cutters, cut dough into shapes. Place cutouts 1 inch apart on an ungreased cookie sheet. If desired, sprinkle with pearl or colored sugars. (Reroll scraps of dough only once. Overworking dough blurs the colors.) Repeat with the second ball of dough.

4 Bake cookies in a 375°F oven for 7 to 8 minutes or until edges are firm and bottoms are very lightly browned. Transfer cookies to a wire rack; cool. Makes about 54 cookies.

CARAMEL APPLE PIE

USE MODERATELY TART APPLES, SUCH AS JONATHANS OR NORTHERN
SPYS, FOR THIS VARIATION OF AMERICA'S FAVORITE PIE.

WHAT YOU'LL NEED

- ★ *1 recipe Pastry for Single-Crust Pie*
- ★ *½ cup sugar*
- ★ *3 tablespoons all-purpose flour*
- ★ *1 teaspoon ground cinnamon*
- ★ *⅛ teaspoon salt*
- ★ *6 cups thinly sliced peeled cooking apples*
- ★ *1 recipe Crumb Topping*
- ★ *½ cup chopped pecans*
- ★ *¼ cup caramel ice cream topping*

HERE'S HOW

1 Prepare Pastry for Single-Crust Pie. On a lightly floured surface, roll out dough to a 12-inch circle. Transfer pastry to a 9-inch pie plate. Ease pastry into pie plate, being careful not to stretch pastry. Trim; crimp edge as desired.

2 In a large mixing bowl stir together sugar, flour, cinnamon, and salt. Add apple slices and gently toss until coated. Transfer apple mixture to the pastry-lined pie plate. Sprinkle Crumb Topping over apple mixture.

3 To prevent overbrowning, cover edge of pie with foil. Bake in a 375°F oven for 25 minutes. Remove foil. Bake for 25 to 30 minutes more or until top is golden. Remove from oven; sprinkle pie with pecans, then drizzle with caramel topping. Cool on a wire rack. Makes 8 servings.

Pastry for Single-Crust Pie: In a bowl stir together 1¼ cups all-purpose flour and ¼ teaspoon salt. Using a pastry blender, cut in ⅓ cup shortening until pieces are pea-size. Using 4 to 5 tablespoons cold water total, sprinkle 1 tablespoon of water at a time over the flour mixture, tossing with a fork until all of the dough is moistened. Form dough into a ball.

Crumb Topping: Stir together 1 cup packed brown sugar, ½ cup all-purpose flour, and ½ cup quick-cooking rolled oats. Using a pastry blender, cut in ½ cup butter or margarine until the topping mixture resembles coarse crumbs.

AMERICAKE

INSTEAD OF USING A SHAPED PAN, USE A LITTLE INGENUITY TO CUSTOM MAKE A PAN IN THE SHAPE OF THE UNITED STATES.

WHAT YOU'LL NEED

- ★ *Large piece of cardboard (at least 15×10 inches)*
- ★ *Batter for a 2-layer cake*
- ★ *2 cups creamy white frosting (use creamy white frosting mix for a 2-layer cake)*
- ★ *1 tube red decorator icing and plastic ribbon tip*
- ★ *Fresh blueberries*

HERE'S HOW

1 To transfer the design, *opposite*, draw a 15×10-inch rectangle onto a large piece of cardboard. Divide the rectangle into 24 squares by drawing horizontal and vertical lines 2½ inches apart. Working several squares at a time, mark the large grid exactly where the outline of the nation intersects each line on the grid, *opposite*. Connect the marks on the large grid with a continuous line, following the outline on the grid. Cut out the design.

2 To make the foil pan, cover the cardboard shape with foil. Tear off about four more sheets of foil that are 12 inches wide and 16 inches long. Fold each in half crosswise to 12×8 inches, then to 12×4 inches, and a third time to make 12×2-inch strips. Snip or tear ½-inch-long notches on one side of each strip at 1-inch intervals.

Folding notched edges under cardboard base, fit strips along the cardboard with the foil extending upward 1½ inches. Tape the strips of foil to the underside of the cardboard base and to each other.

3 Grease and flour the bottom and sides of the foil pan. Place in a 15×10×1-inch baking pan. Pour batter into the foil pan and bake in a 350°F oven for about 30 minutes or until a toothpick inserted in center comes out clean. Cool on wire rack. Remove foil strips, leaving cake on cardboard.

4 Frost sides and top of cake. With a toothpick, mark a box in upper left corner of cake. With red decorator icing and ribbon tip, make stripes across top and down sides of cake, avoiding marked corner of cake. Place rows of blueberries in the corner. Makes 12 servings.

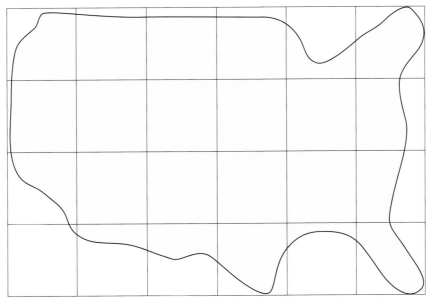

Americake Pattern   1 Square = 2¹/₂ Inches

A LOOK BACK

A Salute to Patriotic Souvenirs

Whether on duty in the United States or abroad, men and women in uniform often think of their families back home. Hankies, frames, and banks were common souvenirs that were sent or brought home in years past. These treasures were cherished at the time and continue to bring joy to the generations that follow.

Items that show loyalty and love for the country never go out of style and blend in wonderfully with today's expressive decorating styles. The most important thing about displaying patriotic souvenirs is to do it tastefully and creatively. Combine favorite family pieces with red, white, and blue glassware or fabrics.

SWEET POTATO SHORTCAKES

TOTE THIS SWEET POTATO VERSION OF THE OLD-FASHIONED CLASSIC TO YOUR NEXT FAMILY OUTING, AND YOU'RE SURE TO GET A PICNIC BASKETFUL OF HIP HIP HOORAYS!

WHAT YOU'LL NEED

★ *1 16-ounce can sweet potatoes (syrup pack)*
★ *½ cup milk*
★ *2 tablespoons margarine or butter, melted*
★ *2½ cups packaged biscuit mix*
★ *2 tablespoons sugar*
★ *¼ teaspoon ground cinnamon*
★ *1½ to 2 quarts fresh strawberries,* red raspberries, blackberries, and/or blueberries*
★ *3 tablespoons sugar*
★ *1 to 1½ cups whipping cream*
★ *2 tablespoons sugar*

HERE'S HOW

1 Grease a large baking sheet. Set aside. Chill a medium mixing bowl and the beaters of an electric mixer.

2 Drain sweet potatoes, reserving 2 tablespoons of the syrup. Mash enough of the sweet potatoes to make ½ cup. (Cover and refrigerate any remaining sweet potatoes and syrup to heat later as a side dish.)

3 In a medium mixing bowl stir together the mashed sweet potatoes, the reserved syrup, the milk, and melted margarine or butter. Sprinkle the biscuit mix, 2 tablespoons sugar, and cinnamon over sweet potato mixture; stir just until dough clings together. (The dough might have some lumps and should be thick.)

4 Drop dough onto the prepared baking sheet in 8 equal portions. Bake in a 425°F oven about 12 minutes or until golden brown. Transfer to a wire rack and allow to cool slightly.

5 Meanwhile, in a large mixing bowl combine fresh berries and the 3 tablespoons sugar. Set aside. In the chilled mixing bowl beat the whipped cream and the 2 tablespoons sugar with an electric mixer on medium speed until soft peaks form (tips curl).

6 To serve, split each shortcake in half crosswise; place bottom halves on 8 dessert plates. Top with some of the berries and some of the whipped cream. Place a shortcake top on each serving. Makes 8 servings.

*Note: If desired, slice the strawberries.

"Americanism is a question of principle, of purpose, of idealism, or character; it is not a matter of birthplace or creed or line of descent."

— THEODORE ROOSEVELT, 1909

FOR-THE-GLORY PIE

WHO COULD RESIST A FRESH BLACKBERRY PIE, ESPECIALLY ONE WITH A LAYER OF SWEETENED SOUR CREAM AND A BUTTERY CRUMB TOPPING? KEEP THIS RECIPE HANDY TO SHARE A FAVORITE AMERICAN PIE.

WHAT YOU'LL NEED

* ★ *1 9-inch unbaked pie shell*
* ★ *¾ to 1 cup sugar*
* ★ *1 8-ounce carton dairy sour cream*
* ★ *3 tablespoons all-purpose flour*
* ★ *¼ teaspoon salt*
* ★ *4 cups fresh blackberries*
* ★ *¼ cup fine dry bread crumbs*
* ★ *2 tablespoons sugar*
* ★ *1 tablespoon butter or margarine, melted*

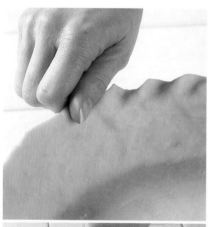

HERE'S HOW

1 Preheat the oven to 450°F. Line the bottom of a pastry-lined 9-inch pie plate with a double thickness of foil. Bake in the 450°F oven for 5 minutes. Remove the foil and bake for 5 minutes more. Remove the pie shell from the oven and cool slightly. Reduce the oven temperature to 375°F.

2 Meanwhile, in a small bowl stir together the ¾ to 1 cup sugar, the sour cream, flour, and salt until combined. Set aside.

3 Place the blackberries in the prebaked pastry shell. Spread the sour cream mixture evenly over the berries as shown, *below left.*

4 In a small bowl, stir together the bread crumbs, the 2 tablespoons sugar, and the melted butter or margarine. Sprinkle the bread crumb mixture on the sour cream mixture.

5 Cover the edge of the pie with foil and bake in the 375°F oven for 25 minutes. Remove the foil. Bake for 20 to 25 minutes more or until the top of the pie is golden and the berry mixture bubbles slightly. Makes 8 servings.

Tips from Our Kitchen

* ★ Use fresh blackberries for this recipe; frozen berries don't work well because they release too much juice as they thaw. However, you could substitute other fresh berries, such as blueberries or raspberries.
* ★ Fine dry bread crumbs are easy to make. For ¼ cup of crumbs, place one slice of dried or lightly toasted bread in a plastic bag and crush it with a rolling pin.
* ★ Pie crust edges are usually fluted by pressing the dough with the forefinger of one hand against the thumb and forefinger of the other hand. To make a rope-shape edge, press the dough between the thumb and a bent forefinger as shown, *top left.*
* ★ An easy way to cover just the edge of the pie with foil is to cut a large circle from the center of a 12-inch foil square.

BERRIES & CREAM

PLEDGE YOUR ALLEGIANCE TO THIS FRUIT-FILLED FLAG LAYERED WITH RICH WHIPPING CREAM.

WHAT YOU'LL NEED

★ *½ cup apple jelly*
★ *1½ cups fresh blueberries*
★ *4 cups fresh strawberries, similar in size, with stems removed*
★ *1 cup whipping cream*
★ *2 tablespoons sugar*
★ *½ teaspoon finely shredded orange peel*
★ *½ teaspoon vanilla*
★ *⅓ cup dairy sour cream*

HERE'S HOW

1 In a small saucepan cook and stir apple jelly over medium heat until melted; cool. Toss blueberries with half of the jelly.

2 On a large rectangular platter or tray (about 13×9 inches) arrange blueberries in upper left-hand corner in a square. Place strawberries, stem side down, in horizontal rows (resembling a flag), leaving about 1 inch between each row for whipped cream filling. With a pastry brush, brush strawberries with remaining jelly.

3 For the whipped cream filling, in a chilled mixing bowl combine whipping cream, sugar, finely shredded orange peel, and vanilla. Beat with chilled beaters of an electric mixer on medium speed until soft peaks form (tips curl). Fold in sour cream. Place filling in a pastry bag fitted with a large, grooved tip.

4 Pipe the whipped cream filling in rows between the strawberries. Serve immediately or cover and chill for up to 2 hours. Makes 10 to 12 servings.

RASPBERRY STAR DESSERT

DRESS UP YOUR RED, WHITE, AND BLUE BUFFET TABLE WITH A SPECTACULAR FROSTED GELATIN.

WHAT YOU'LL NEED

★ *1 6-ounce package raspberry-flavored gelatin*
★ *2 cups boiling water*
★ *1 16-ounce jar applesauce*
★ *1 10-ounce package frozen red raspberries in syrup, thawed*
★ *½ cup tiny marshmallows*
★ *1 to 2 tablespoons milk*
★ *¼ cup dairy sour cream*
★ *5-cup star-shape gelatin mold*

HERE'S HOW

1 Dissolve gelatin in boiling water. Let stand about 30 minutes to cool. Stir in the applesauce and raspberries with their syrup. Pour into a 5- to 6-cup mold. Cover and chill in the refrigerator for 2 to 3 hours or until firm. Remove from mold.★

2 For drizzle, in a small saucepan combine marshmallows and milk. Cook and stir over low heat until marshmallows are melted. Remove from heat; let stand about 10 minutes. Stir in the sour cream.

3 Place mixture in a clear plastic bag. Snip off a corner of the bag and drizzle the mixture over the salad. Chill in refrigerator about 1 hour or until firm. Garnish the salad with the drizzle up to 4 hours before serving. Makes 8 servings.

Frosted Raspberry Salad: Prepare salad as above, except pour gelatin mixture into an 8×8×2-inch pan. Cover and chill salad as directed. For topping, combine 2 cups tiny marshmallows and ⅓ cup milk. Cook and stir over low heat until the marshmallows are melted. Remove from heat and let stand for 10 minutes. Stir in one 8-ounce carton dairy sour cream. Spread over the gelatin. Chill at least 1 hour or until topping is firm.

Tip From Our Kitchen
★ To unmold gelatin, set mold in a bowl filled with warm water for a few seconds or until edges start to separate from mold; invert over serving plate and remove the mold.

PETITE BERRY PASTRIES

YOU'LL BE PROUD TO SHARE THESE CHOCOLATE-FLAVORED PASTRIES.

WHAT YOU'LL NEED

- ★ *1 package piecrust mix (for 2 crusts)*
- ★ *¼ cup packed brown sugar*
- ★ *⅓ cup chocolate-flavor syrup*
- ★ *1¼ cup whipping cream*
- ★ *⅓ cup granulated sugar*
- ★ *¾ cup dairy sour cream*
- ★ *2 tablespoons orange liqueur*
- ★ *1½ cups raspberries, blackberries, blueberries, or sliced strawberries*
- ★ *Orange peel curls (optional)*
- ★ *Powdered sugar (optional)*

HERE'S HOW

1 In a large bowl combine pie crust mix and brown sugar; add syrup. Stir together until mixture forms a ball. On a lightly floured surface, roll dough to ⅛ inch thickness. Using a 3-inch cookie or biscuit cutter, cut into rounds. Reroll trimmings as necessary to make 30 pastry rounds. Transfer rounds to an ungreased baking sheet. Bake in a 400°F oven about 6 minutes or until set. Transfer to a wire rack and cool.

2 In a chilled large bowl combine the whipping cream and granulated sugar. Beat with chilled beaters of an electric mixer on medium speed until soft peaks form (tips curl). Fold in sour cream. Spoon whipped cream mixture into a large self-sealing plastic bag; seal bag. Carefully cut a small hole in one corner of the bag.

3 To assemble, pipe about 3 tablespoons of the whipped cream mixture onto a pastry round. Repeat layers. Place a third pastry on top. Repeat to make a total of 6 stacks.* Cover stacks and remaining whipped cream mixture with plastic wrap; chill 4 to 6 hours. (Chilling softens the pastry, making it easier to eat.)

4 To serve, drizzle liqueur over berries; toss gently. Top stacks with remaining whipped cream mixture. Spoon some of the berries on top of each serving. If desired, garnish with orange peel curls and dust with powdered sugar. Makes 6 servings.

* Note: Wrap and freeze remaining pastry rounds for up to 6 months. Thaw at room temperature to serve.

A LOOK BACK
A Salute to the 4th of July

In honor of Independence Day, bring a touch of Americana into your home. A collection of red, white, and blue outlasts other passing fads and lends itself to timeless decorating. Here are some ideas to get started:

★ In a basket, display items such as sparklers, small statues, and red, white, and blue shredded paper.

★ Choose a photo of a favorite president for the wall.

★ Visit antiques shows, shops, and estate sales to find authentic artifacts. Don't rule out contemporary interpretations, however; crafts shows and specialty boutiques harbor beautiful reproductions.

HOME RUN PIE

✦

CARAMEL-COATED POPCORN AND PEANUTS MAKE THIS SWEET TREAT A FAMILY FAVORITE ALL SUMMER LONG.

WHAT YOU'LL NEED

★ *1 recipe Pastry for Single-Crust Pie (see recipe, below)*
★ *2 eggs, slightly beaten*
★ *⅔ cup light-colored corn syrup*
★ *½ cup sugar*
★ *¼ cup margarine or butter, melted*
★ *1 teaspoon vanilla*
★ *¾ cup lightly salted dry-roasted peanuts*
★ *1½ to 2 cups caramel-coated popcorn and peanuts*

HERE'S HOW

1 Preheat oven to 350°F. Prepare pastry for Single-Crust Pie. Divide pastry into 4 portions. On lightly floured surface roll each portion of pastry into a 6-inch circle. Ease each pastry round into a 5-inch individual pie pan. Trim pastry to within ¼ inch of the pie pan edge. Snip star-shape points around edges of crusts with kitchen shears.

2 For filling, in a medium bowl combine eggs, corn syrup, sugar, margarine or butter, and vanilla. Mix well. Stir in dry-roasted peanuts. Place pans on a 15×10×1-inch baking sheet. Divide filling evenly among the pastry shells.

3 Bake for 35 to 40 minutes or until a knife inserted near the center comes out clean.

4 Remove pans from oven. Divide 1½ to 2 cups of the caramel-coated popcorn and peanuts over the 4 pies. Return to oven and bake 3 minutes more. Cool on a wire rack. Refrigerate within 2 hours of cooling. Cover for longer storage. Makes 4 tart-size pies, 8 servings.

Pastry for Single-Crust Pie: Stir together 1¼ cups all-purpose flour and ¼ teaspoon salt. Cut in ⅓ cup shortening until pieces are the size of small peas. Using a total of 4 to 5 tablespoons cold water, sprinkle 1 tablespoon at a time over part of the mixture. Gently toss with a fork. Push to side of bowl. Repeat until all is moistened. Form into a ball.

✦

A LOOK BACK
A Salute to Military Uniform Buttons

Whether you have family heirlooms or a purchased collection, military uniform buttons deserve a place of honor. To display them in your home, here are some great ideas:

★ Sew them onto the cuff of a Christmas stocking.
★ Display the buttons by attaching them to a red, white, and blue pillow, quilt, or tapestry.
★ Place uniform buttons in transparent canning jars.
★ Photocopy the buttons to use in scrapbooking.
★ Sew 5 or 6 vertically or horizontally on wool, then mat and frame.

SALUTING FLAG ETIQUETTE

Treat Old Glory with the respect she deserves using the following guidelines from the Federal Flag Code:

FLAG DOS

★ Display the flag from sunrise to sunset on buildings and outdoor stationary flagstaffs.

★ The flag can be displayed 24 hours a day if the flag is illuminated during the hours of darkness.

★ Pay attention to the position of the union (the blue field). When projecting horizontally or at an angle from a windowsill or front of a building, the union should be at the peak of the staff, unless the flag is at half-staff. When displayed against a wall or in a window, the union should be uppermost and to the flag's own right (the observer's left).

★ When flown at half-staff (the flag is flown at half-staff by order of the President, customarily upon the death of prominent members of the government as a mark of respect), the flag should be raised to the peak for an instant and then lowered to the half-staff position. Just before the flag is lowered for the day, the flag should once again be momentarily hoisted to the peak. To position the flag at half-staff, place the flag half the distance between the top and bottom of the staff.

★ Dispose of a flag that is frayed, tattered, or otherwise inappropriate for display. The flag should be destroyed in a respectful manner, preferably by burning, according to U.S. Code, Title 36, Section 176k, Respect for Flag.

★ If you have a 48-star flag or another historic U.S. flag, you may display it with pride. The 50-star flag is the official flag of the U.S. as designated by President Eisenhower in 1959. There are many historic U.S. flags, and, according to tradition (the Flag Code does not address this issue), they may be displayed as long as they are in good condition (unfrayed, unstained, unsoiled, without rips, tears, or holes). Historic U.S. flags should be treated with the same respect and rituals as the official flag.

★ You can place a symbolic finial on flagstaffs. Finials for flagstaffs are not mentioned in the Flag Code, but, by implication, they are acceptable. The President, the Vice President, and many federal agencies use an eagle finial.

★ An indoor flag may have a fringe (a fringe on an outdoor flag would deteriorate too quickly). The Army has used a fringed flag since 1895.

★ To display the flag on a car, the staff should be attached to the chassis or the right fender. On a float in a parade, the flag may only be displayed from a staff.

★ A flag patch may only be attached to the uniforms of military personnel, firefighters,

police officers, and members of patriotic organizations.

★ Position a lapel flag pin on the left lapel, near the heart.

★ Bunting of blue, white, and red, arranged with blue above, white in the center, and red below, is used to cover a speaker's desk, to drape in front of a platform, or to decorate general interior or exterior spaces. Many flag Web sites and patriotic memorabilia sites carry bunting. Available as ornamental banners, in fans, and by the bolt, the flag is available in traditional cotton, cotton/polyester, and plastic.

FLAG DON'TS

★ Unless you have an all-weather flag (made of nylon, polyester, or treated cotton), the flag should not be displayed during inclement weather.

★ Never display the flag with the union (blue field) down, except as a signal of extreme distress, as in danger to life or property.

★ The flag should not be allowed to touch anything beneath it, such as the ground, floor, water, or merchandise.

★ Carry the flag aloft and floating free, not flat or horizontal.

★ Do not place the flag over the hood, top, sides, or back of vehicle, including a train or boat.

★ Neither the flag nor any part of the flag may be used as a costume or athletic uniform.

★ Do not use the actual flag for apparel, bedding, drapery, or as a ceiling covering.

★ The flag must always fall free and must never be festooned, drawn back or up, or in folds.

★ The flag must not be used to receive, hold, carry, or deliver anything.

★ Don't use the flag for advertising nor attach advertising signs to the flag's staff or halyard.

★ No mark, insignia, letter, word, figure, design, picture, or drawing can be placed on the flag or any part of the flag.

★ No items that are intended for temporary use should be adorned with the flag. The actual flag should not be embroidered, printed, or embossed on cushions, handkerchiefs, napkins, boxes, or anything that will be discarded.

★ Protect your flag—make sure that it is not displayed or stored in a way that would allow the flag to be torn, soiled, or otherwise damaged.

Source: CRS Report for Congress (Congressional Research Service, The Library of Congress), The United States Flag: Federal Law Relating to Display and Associated Questions, John R. Luckey, Legislative Attorney, American Law Division, *updated June 14, 2000.*

INDEX

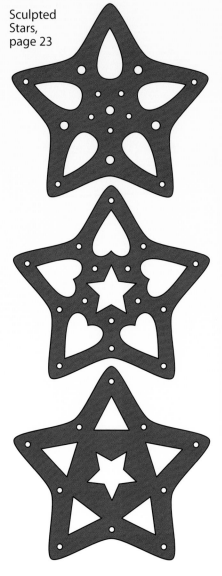

Sculpted Stars, page 23

PILLOW

PILLOW

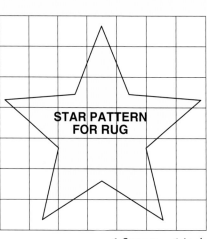

STAR PATTERN FOR RUG

1 Square = 1 Inch

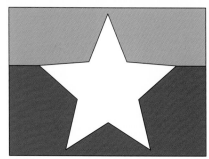

RUG

Razzle-Dazzle Accents, page 26